THE PRINCE

Nicolas Machiavelli

1532 (1st publication)

Dedication

NICOLAS MACHIAVELLI

AT

MAGNIFIQUE LAURENT

SON OF PIERRE DE MÉDICIS

Those who aspire to acquire the good graces of a prince are usually in the habit of offering him, on approaching him, some of the things which they most esteem among those which they possess, or in which they see him most pleased. Thus they often offer him horses, weapons, pieces of gold cloth, precious stones and other similar objects worthy of his greatness.

Desiring therefore to present myself to Your Magnificence with some testimony of my devotion, I have found, in all that belongs to me, nothing more dear and more precious than the knowledge of the actions of men elevated in power, which I have acquired, either by long experience of modern affairs or by assiduous study of those of ancient times, which I have spent a long time thinking about and examining very carefully, and which I have finally written down in a small volume that I dare to address to Your Magnificence today.

Although I regard this work as unworthy of appearing before you, I trust that your indulgence will deign to accept it, when you will consider that the greatest gift I could make you was to give you the means of knowing in a very short time what I learned only in a long course of years, and at the price of much trouble and danger.

I have not adorned this work with grand reasonings, or with pompous and magnificent phrases, or, in a word, with all those foreign finery with which most authors are accustomed to embellish their writings: I wanted my book to draw all its lustre from its own depths, and for the variety of the subject matter and the importance of the subject to be its only pleasure.

Moreover, I would ask that I not be accused of presumption if, as a simple private individual, and even of an inferior rank, I have dared to discuss the government of princes and to give rules for it. Just as those who wish to draw a landscape go down to the plain to obtain the structure and appearance of the mountains and high places, and on the contrary climb to the heights when they have to paint the plains: in the same way, to know the nature of peoples well, it is necessary to be a prince; and to know princes equally well, it is necessary to be a people.

May Your Magnificence therefore accept this modest gift in the same spirit in which I address it to her. If she examines it and reads it with some attention, she will see in it everywhere the extreme desire I have to see her achieve the greatness that fortune and her other qualities promise her. And if Your Magnificence, from the height of her elevation, sometimes lowers her gaze to what is so far below her, she will see how little I have deserved to be the continual victim of an unjust and rigorous fortune.

THE PRINCE[1]

Chapter I How many kinds of principalities there are, and by what means they may be acquired.

All the States, all the dominations which have held and still hold men under their empire, have been and are either republics or principalities.

Principalities are either hereditary or new.

The hereditary ones are those that have long been owned by their prince's family.

The new ones are either completely new, as Milan was for Francesco Sforza, or they are like members added to the hereditary States of the prince who acquired them; such was the kingdom of Naples with regard to the king of Spain.

Moreover, the States acquired in this way were accustomed either to living under a prince or to being free: the acquisition was made with the weapons of others, or by those of the purchaser himself, or by the favour of fortune, or by the ascendancy of virtue.

CHAPTER II. Hereditary principalities.

I will not deal here with republics[2], because I have already spoken at length about them elsewhere: I will deal only with principalities; and, continuing with the distinctions I have just made, I will examine how, in these various hypotheses, princes can conduct themselves and maintain themselves.

It is enough for the prince not to overstep the bounds set by his ancestors, and to temporise with events. Also, even if he is gifted with only ordinary ability, he will be able to hold on to the throne, unless an irresistible force beyond all foresight topples him from it; but even if he has lost it, the slightest setback suffered by the usurper will make it easy for him to regain it. Italy offers us an example of this in the Duke of Ferrara: if in 1484 he resisted the attacks of the Venetians, and in 1510 those of Pope Julius II, it was only because his family had long been established in his duchy.

In fact, a hereditary prince has far fewer reasons and finds himself far less in need of displeasing his subjects: by the same token, he is far more beloved by them; and, unless extraordinary vices make him hated, they must naturally be fond of him. Moreover, in the age and long continuity of a power, the memory of previous innovations fades; the causes that produced them vanish: there are therefore no more of those kinds of stepping stones that one revolution always leaves to support a second.

CHAPTER III. Mixed principalities.

It's in a new principality that all the difficulties come together.

First of all, if it is not entirely new, but added like a member to another, so that together they form a body that can be called mixed, there is a first source of change in a natural difficulty inherent in all new principalities : It is that men like to change masters in the hope of improving their lot; that this hope puts arms in their hands against the present government; but that afterwards experience shows them that they were mistaken and that they have only made their situation worse: an inevitable consequence of another natural necessity in which the new prince usually finds himself to burden his subjects, both with the upkeep of his armies, and with an infinity of other burdens that new conquests bring with them.

The position of this prince is such that, on the one hand, he has as enemies all those whose interests he has hurt by seizing this principality; and that, on the other, he cannot retain the friendship and loyalty of those who facilitated his entry, either because he is unable to satisfy them as much as they had promised, or because it does not suit him to use against them those heroic remedies which gratitude forces him to abstain from; for, however powerful a prince may be through his armies, he always needs, to enter a country, to be helped by the favour of the inhabitants.

This is why Louis XII, King of France, took control of Milan in an instant, which he also lost, and why at first the forces of Lodovico Sforza alone were enough to wrest it from him. Indeed, the inhabitants who had opened the gates to him, seeing their hopes deluded and frustrated by the advantages they had expected, could not bear the disgust of a new domination.

It is quite true that when countries that have rebelled in this way are reconquered, they are more difficult to lose: the conqueror, taking advantage of this rebellion, proceeds with less restraint in the means of ensuring his conquest, either by punishing the guilty, or by seeking out suspects, or by fortifying all the weak parts of his States.

This is also why, in order to take Milan from France for the first time, it was enough for Duke Lodovico to stir up a few rumours on the borders of this province. To make him lose it a second time, it was necessary for everyone to unite against him, for his armies to be completely dispersed, and for them to be driven out of Italy; which could only happen for the reasons I have already explained: nevertheless, he lost this province both the first and the second time.

As for the second, it is worth dwelling on it a little more, and examining the means that Louis XII could use, and which any other prince could use in similar circumstances, to hold on to his new conquests a little better than the king of France did.

I therefore say that the States conquered in order to be united with those which have long belonged to the conqueror, are or are not in the same region as the latter, and that they have or do not have the same language.

In the first case, it is easy to keep them, especially when they are not accustomed to living in freedom: to possess them safely, it is enough to have extinguished the race of the prince who was the master; and if, in everything else, they are left in their old way of being, as customs are the same, the subjects soon live peacefully. It is in this way that Brittany, Burgundy, Gascony and Normandy have remained united with France for so many years; and even if there were some differences in language, as habits and customs are similar, these united States could easily come to an agreement. It is only necessary for the person who becomes their possessor to pay attention to two things if he wants to keep them: one is, as I have just said, to extinguish the race of the former prince; the other is not to alter either the laws or the method of taxation: in this way, the old principality and the new one will, in a very short time, be a single body.

But in the second case, i.e. when the states acquired are in a country other than the one to which they are united, when they have neither the same language, nor the same customs, nor the same institutions, then the difficulties are excessive, and great happiness and great skill are needed to keep them. One of the best and most effective means would be for the victor to establish his personal residence there: nothing would make possession more secure and lasting. This is also the course taken by the

Turk with regard to Greece, which, despite all his other measures, he would certainly never have been able to keep if he had not determined to come and live there.

When he lives in the country, the new prince sees disorders as they arise, and can put a stop to them at once. If he is far away, he does not know about them until they are already serious and he can no longer remedy them.

Moreover, his presence prevents his officers from devouring the province; and, in any case, it is a source of satisfaction for the inhabitants to have, so to speak, their recourse to the prince himself at hand. They also have more reason either to love him, if they want to be good and loyal subjects, or to fear him, if they want to be bad. Finally, a foreigner who would like to attack this state is much less likely to venture in; especially as the prince is resident there, it is very difficult to take him away.

The next best thing is to establish colonies in one or two places that are like the keys to the country: otherwise, you are obliged to maintain a large number of men-at-arms and infantry there. The establishment of colonies is not very costly for the prince; he can send and maintain them at no cost, or at least at almost no cost; he only hurts those from whom he takes their fields and houses to give them to the new inhabitants. Now the men thus offended, being only a very small part of the population, and remaining scattered and poor, can never become harmful; while all those not affected by his rigour remain calm for this reason alone; moreover, they dare not behave badly for fear that they too might be robbed. In a word, these colonies, which are so inexpensive, are more loyal and less of a burden to their subjects; and, as I said earlier, those who suffer from them, being poor and scattered, are incapable of doing harm. It follows that, when it comes to offending a man, it must be done in such a way that we cannot fear his vengeance[3].

But if, instead of sending colonies, we decide to maintain troops, the resulting expenditure increases without limit, and all the State's income is used up in guarding it. So the acquisition becomes a real loss, which hurts the inhabitants all the more because they are hurt more; because they all have to suffer, as does the State, from the housing and movement of troops.

Now, since everyone is exposed to this burden, they all become enemies of the prince, and enemies capable of causing harm, since they remain reviled in their homes. Such a guard is therefore in any case as useless as that of the colonies would be profitable.

But that is not all. When the conquered state is in a country other than the conqueror's hereditary state, there are many other concerns that the conqueror must not neglect: he must make himself the ruler and protector of the least powerful neighbouring princes in the country, work to weaken those of them who are strongest, and prevent, under any pretext, a foreigner as powerful as himself from being introduced there; an introduction that will certainly be favoured, because this foreigner cannot fail to be called upon by all those who are dissatisfied by ambition or fear. This is how the Romans were introduced into Greece by the Etolians, and how the entrance to all the other countries they entered was opened to them by the inhabitants.

Here is how things work: as soon as a powerful foreigner enters a country, all the less powerful princes there attach themselves to him and favour his enterprise, aroused by the envy they harbour against those whose power was greater than their own. He therefore has no trouble winning over these less powerful princes, who all hasten to form a single mass with the State he has just conquered. He must only take care that they do not become too strong or too authoritative: with their help and his own means, he will easily succeed in lowering the most powerful and making himself the sole arbiter of the region. If he neglects to behave properly in these circumstances, he will soon lose the fruit of his conquest; and as long as he keeps it, he will experience all kinds of difficulties and disgust.

The Romans, in the countries of which they became masters, never neglected anything that had to be done. They sent colonies there, they protected the weakest without increasing their power; they brought down the great; they did not allow powerful foreigners to acquire the slightest credit there. I will give just one example as proof of this. Let us see what they did in Greece: there they supported the Achaeans and the Aetolians; there they brought down the kingdom of Macedonia, they drove out Antiochus; but whatever services they had received from the Achaeans and the Aetolians, they did not allow these two peoples to increase their

States; All Philip's appeals could not persuade them to be his friends, without him losing something; and all Antiochus' power could never make them consent to his possessing the slightest state in those regions.

In these circumstances, the Romans acted as wise princes should, whose duty it is to think not only of present disorders but also of those that may arise, in order to remedy them by all the means that prudence can indicate. It is, in fact, by foreseeing them from a distance that it is much easier to remedy them; whereas if they have been allowed to develop, the time is past and the evil becomes incurable. It is then as in the case of etisia, which doctors say is a disease that is easy to cure but difficult to know about, and which, once it has progressed, becomes easy to know about but difficult to cure. This is what happens in all affairs of state: when the illness is foreseen from afar, which is only possible for men of great sagacity, it is soon cured; but when, for lack of light, it is only seen when it strikes all eyes, the cure is impossible. The Romans, who knew how to foresee all inconveniences from afar, always remedied them in time, and never let them run their course in order to avoid a war: they knew full well that war can never be avoided, and that if it is postponed, it is to the enemy's advantage. This is why, although they could have avoided it at the time, they wanted to wage war against Philip and Antiochus in Greece itself, so as not to have to fight against them in Italy. They never tasted those words that we constantly hear coming out of the mouths of wise men today: Enjoy the benefits of time; they preferred the benefits of value and prudence; for time also drives everything before it, and brings in its wake good as well as evil, evil as well as good.

But let us return to France and examine whether it did any of the things I have just described. I will speak only of King Louis XII, and not of Charles VIII, because the former having held on to his conquests in Italy for longer, we were able to get a better idea of his way of proceeding. It must have been clear that he did the very opposite of what was needed to preserve a state quite different from the one to which it was intended to be added.

King Louis XII was introduced to Italy by the ambition of the Venetians, who wanted, through his arrival, to acquire half the duchy of Lombardy. I do not wish to criticise the king's decision: since he wanted to set foot in Italy, where he had no friends and whose doors had been closed to him by the conduct of Charles VIII, he was forced to embrace the first friendships he could find; and the decision he took could even have been a good one, had he not made any other mistakes in the rest of his expeditions. Thus, having conquered Lombardy, he soon regained the reputation that Charles had caused him to lose: Genoa submitted; the Florentines became his allies; the Marquis of Mantua, the Duke of Ferrara, the Bentivogli family, the Lady of Forli, the lords of Faenza, Pesaro, Rimini, Camerino, Piombino, the Lucchese, the Pisans, the Sienese, all ran to his friendship. The Venetians also had to recognise how imprudent they had been when, in order to acquire two cities in Lombardy, they had made the King of France sovereign over two thirds of Italy.

In such circumstances, it would undoubtedly have been easy for Louis XII to retain all his ascendancy in this region, if he had been able to put into practice the rules of conduct set out above; if he had protected and defended those many friends, who, weak and trembling some before the Church, others before the Venetians, were obliged to remain loyal to him, and by means of whom he could easily secure all those who still had some power left.

But he had scarcely arrived in Milan when he did quite the opposite, helping Pope Alexander VI to seize the Romagna. He did not understand that he was weakening himself, by depriving himself of the friends who had thrown themselves into his arms, and that he was enlarging the Church, by adding to the spiritual power, which already gave it so much authority, an equally considerable temporal power.

This first mistake led to so many others that the king himself had to come to Italy to put a stop to Alexander's ambition and prevent him from making himself master of Tuscany.

And that was not all. Not content with having thus enlarged the Church, and deprived himself of his friends, Louis, burning to possess the kingdom of Naples, determined to share it with the king of Spain : so that, while he was the sole arbiter of Italy, he himself introduced into it a rival to whom all the ambitious and all the discontented could have recourse; and when he could leave on the throne a king who considered himself fortunate to be his tributary, he overthrew him to place on it a prince who was in a position to oust him himself.

The desire to acquire is undoubtedly an ordinary and natural thing; and anyone who indulges in it, when he has the means, is praised rather than blamed: but to form the intention without being able to carry it out is to incur blame and to commit an error. If France had sufficient forces to attack the kingdom of Naples, it should have done so; if it did not, it should not have shared it.

If the division of Lombardy with the Venetians could be excused, it was because it gave France the means to gain a foothold in Italy; but that of the kingdom of Naples, not having been similarly determined by necessity, remains without excuse. Thus Louis XII had made five mistakes in Italy: he had ruined the weak, he had increased the power of a powerful man, he had introduced a very powerful foreign prince, he had not come to stay and had not sent colonies there.

However, as long as he lived, these five faults might not have become fatal to him, had he not committed a sixth, that of wanting to strip the Venetians of their States. Indeed, it would have been good and necessary to weaken them, had he not also enlarged the Church and called Spain into Italy; but having done both, he should never have consented to their ruin, because, as long as they had remained powerful, they would have prevented the king's enemies from attacking Lombardy. Indeed, on the one hand, they would only have consented on condition that they became masters of that country; on the other, no one would have wanted to take it from France to give it to them; and finally, it would have seemed too dangerous to attack the French and the Venetians together.

If I were told that Louis had only abandoned the Romagna to Pope Alexander, and shared the kingdom of Naples with Spain, to avoid war, I would reply as I have already said, that one must never, for such a motive, allow disorder to persist; for one does not avoid war, one only delays it to one's own disadvantage.

If it were still alleged that the king had promised the pope to conquer this province for him, in order to obtain the dissolution of his marriage and the cardinal's hat for the archbishop of Rouen (afterwards called the Cardinal of Amboise), I would reply with what will be said below, concerning the promises of princes, and the manner in which they must keep them.

Louis XII therefore lost Lombardy because he did not comply with any of the rules followed by all those who, having acquired a State, wish to keep it. There is no miracle in that; it is a very simple and natural thing.I was in Nantes at the time when the Valentinois (as Caesar Borgia, son of Pope Alexander VI, was then called) was taking control of the Romagna: the Cardinal d'Amboise, with whom I was discussing this event, having told me that the Italians understood nothing about affairs of war, I replied that the French understood nothing about affairs of state, because, if they had understood anything, they would not have allowed the Church to expand to such an extent. Experience, in fact, has shown that the greatness of the Church and that of Spain in Italy were the work of France, and then the cause of its ruin in that region. From this we can also draw a general rule that rarely, if ever, deceives: that the prince who makes another powerful is working to his own ruin; for this power is produced either by skill or by force: and both of these two causes make anyone who uses them suspect of the person for whom they are used.

CHAPTER IV. Why the States of Darius, conquered by Alexander, did not revolt against the successors of the conqueror after his death.

When you consider how difficult it is to keep a newly conquered state, you may be surprised at what happened after the death of Alexander the Great. In a few short years, this prince had made himself master of the whole of Asia, and he died almost immediately. It was likely that the empire would take advantage of his death to revolt; nevertheless, his successors held on to it, and they experienced no difficulty other than that which arose between them from their own ambition.

To this I would reply that all the principalities known to us, and of which there is some memory, are governed in two different ways: either by a prince and slaves, who help him to govern, as ministers, only by a grace and a concession that he is willing to make to them; or by a prince and barons, who hold their rank not from the favour of the sovereign, but from the seniority of their race; who have states and subjects who belong to them and recognise them as lords, and who have a natural affection for them.

In principalities governed by a prince and by slaves, the prince has much greater authority, since throughout the extent of his States he alone is recognised as superior, and if the subjects obey any other, they regard him only as their minister or officer, to whom they feel no personal attachment.

Turkey and the kingdom of France can be cited today as examples of both types of government.

The whole of Turkey is ruled by a single master, to whom all the other Turks are slaves, and who, having divided his empire into several sangiacs, sends governors who he revokes and changes at his whim.

In France, on the other hand, the king is surrounded by a host of lords of ancient race, recognised as such by their subjects, who are loved by them, and who enjoy prerogatives that the king could not take away from them without danger to himself.

If we reflect on the nature of these two forms of government, we will see that it is difficult to conquer the empire of the Turks, but that once conquered, it is very easy to keep it.

The difficulty of conquering the Turkish empire stems from the fact that the conqueror can never be called upon by the great men of this monarchy, nor can he hope to be helped in his enterprise by the rebellion of some of those who surround the monarch. I have already indicated the reasons for this. All of them, in fact, being equally his slaves and equally indebted to him for their wealth, it is very difficult to corrupt them; and even if you succeeded, you would have to expect little benefit, because they cannot lead the people into revolt. Anyone wishing to attack the Turks must therefore expect to find them united against him, have little hope of being helped by internal disorder, and rely little on anything but his own strength.

But once the conquest has been made and the monarch defeated in pitched battle, so that his armies can no longer be replenished, the only thing left to fear is his race, which, once extinguished, leaves no one to fear, because there is no one left who retains any ascendancy over the people; so that if, before the victory, there was nothing to hope for from the subjects, in the same way, once it has been won, there is nothing to fear from them.

It is quite different in States governed like France. It may be easy to get in by winning over some of the great men of the kingdom; and there are always some who are dissatisfied, who are eager for novelty and change, and who can indeed, for the reasons I have already mentioned, open up the kingdom's roads and facilitate victory; but, if it is then a question of holding on, it is then that the conqueror encounters all sorts of difficulties, both on the part of those who have helped him and on the part of those he has had to oppress.

There, it is not enough for him to extinguish the prince's race, for there always remain a host of lords who will put themselves at the head of new movements; and as it is neither possible for him to satisfy them all nor to destroy them, he will lose his conquest as soon as the opportunity arises.

Now, if we consider the nature of the government of Darius, we will find that it resembled that of Turkey: so Alexander had to fight against all the forces of the empire, and he first had to defeat the monarch in the middle of the campaign; but, after his victory and the death of Darius, the victor, for the reasons I have explained, remained the tranquil possessor of his conquest. And if his successors had remained united, they would have enjoyed their conquest equally in the bosom of rest and pleasure; for throughout the empire only the troubles that they themselves caused arose.

But as for states governed like France, it is far from possible to maintain such tranquillity. Proof of this can be seen in the frequent uprisings against the Romans in Spain, Gaul and Greece. These rebellions were caused by the numerous principalities in these regions, whose mere memory, for as long as it remained, was a source of trouble and anxiety for the victors. It was not until the power and duration of Roman domination had extinguished the memory of these principalities that their owners were finally at peace.

There is even more. When the Romans were subsequently at war with each other, each of the parties was able to win and have for itself those ancient principalities where it had the most influence, and which, after the extinction of the race of their princes, knew no other domination than that of Rome.

Anyone who has reflected on all these considerations will no doubt no longer be surprised at the ease with which Alexander maintained himself in Asia, and at the difficulty, on the contrary, that others, such as Pyrrhus, had in preserving their conquests. This was not due to the greater or lesser skill of the conqueror, but to the different nature of the conquered states.

CHAPTER V. How to govern States or principalities which, before the conquest, lived under their own laws.

When the conquered States are, as I have said, accustomed to living free under their own laws, the conqueror may proceed in three ways to maintain himself there: the first is to destroy them; the second, to go and reside there in person; the third, to leave them their laws, confining himself to demanding tribute, and to establishing there a small government which will keep them in obedience and fidelity : which such a government will undoubtedly do; for, holding all its existence from the conqueror, it knows that it cannot preserve it without his support and protection; moreover, a State accustomed to freedom is more easily governed by its own citizens than by others.

The Spartans and Romans can serve as an example here.

The Spartans held on to Athens and Thebes, entrusting only a small number of people with power there; nevertheless, they subsequently lost them. The Romans, in order to retain control of Capua, Carthage and Numance, destroyed them but did not lose them. They wanted to use them in Greece like the Spartans: they gave it back its freedom and left it its own laws, but this did not succeed. In order to hold on to this land, they had to destroy a large number of cities, which was the only sure way to possess it. And, in fact, whoever, having conquered a State accustomed to living in freedom, does not destroy it, must expect to be destroyed by it. In such a State, rebellion is constantly aroused by the name of liberty and by the memory of old institutions, which neither the length of time nor the benefits of a new master can ever erase from its memory. Whatever precautions you take, whatever you do, if you do not dissolve the State, if you do not disperse its inhabitants, you will find them, at the first opportunity, recalling, invoking their freedom, their lost institutions, and striving to regain them. This is how Pisa broke the Florentine yoke after more than a hundred years of slavery.

But it is very different for countries accustomed to living under a prince. If the race of this prince is once extinct, the inhabitants, already moulded to obedience, unable to agree in the choice of a new master, and not knowing how to live free, are in no hurry to take up arms; so that the conqueror can without difficulty either win them over or secure them. In republics, on the other hand, there is a principle of life that is far more active, a hatred that is far more profound, a desire for vengeance that is far more ardent, which does not and cannot leave the memory of ancient liberty in peace for a moment.

CHAPTER VI. New principalities acquired by arms and by the skill of the purchaser.

Don't be surprised if, in speaking of completely new principalities of princes and states, I cite some very great examples. Men almost always walk down paths that have already been trodden; they almost always act by imitation; but it is hardly possible for them to follow exactly in the footsteps of those who have gone before them, or to match the virtue of those they have set out to imitate. They must therefore take the greatest figures as their guides and models, so that even if they do not rise to the same degree of greatness and glory, they can at least reproduce its fragrance. They should do as those prudent archers do, who, judging that the proposed goal is beyond the range of their bow and their strength, aim even further, so that their arrow reaches the point they wish to reach.

First of all, I would say that, in the case of completely new principalities, the greater or lesser difficulty of maintaining one's position depends on the greater or lesser skill of the person who has acquired it. There is reason to believe that a man who has risen from the ranks of a private individual to the rank of prince is either a skilful man or one aided by fortune: to which I would add that the less he owes to fortune, the better he will be able to maintain himself. Moreover, such a prince, having no other states, is obliged to come and live in his own country, which further reduces the difficulty.

But, in any case, to speak first of those who became princes by their own virtue and not by fortune, the most remarkable are: Moses, Cyrus, Romulus, Theseus, and a few others like them[4].

Although we should not reason much about Moses, because he was only a simple executor of God's orders, there is always reason to admire him, if only because of the grace which made him worthy of conversing with the Divinity. But if we consider the actions and conduct of Cyrus and the other conquerors and founders of kingdoms, we will admire them all equally, and we will find great conformity between them and Moses, even though the latter was led by such a great master.

We shall see first of all that all they owed to fortune was the opportunity that provided them with the material to which they could give the form they deemed appropriate. Without this opportunity, the great qualities of their souls would have remained useless; but also, without these great qualities, the opportunity would have presented itself in vain. It was not until Moses found the Israelites enslaved and oppressed in Egypt that the desire to escape from slavery determined them to follow him. For Romulus to become the founder and king of Rome, he had to be taken out of Alba and exposed immediately after his birth. Cyrus needed to find the Persians dissatisfied with the domination of the Medes, and the Medes softened and effeminate by the delights of a long peace. Finally, Theseus would not have shown his worth if the Athenians had not been dispersed. The happiness of these great men was therefore born of opportunity; but it was through their skill that they knew how to seize it and put it to good use for the great prosperity and glory of their homeland. Those who, like them, and by the same means, become princes, will acquire their principality only with great difficulty, but they will maintain it easily.

In this respect, their difficulties will arise above all from the new institutions and new forms that they will be obliged to introduce in order to found their government and ensure their safety; and it should be noted that there is no undertaking more difficult to carry out, more uncertain as to success, and more dangerous than that of introducing new institutions. Those who embark on it have as enemies all those who benefited from the old institutions, and they find only lukewarm defenders in those for whom the new ones would be useful. This lukewarmness, moreover, comes from two causes: the first is the fear they have of their opponents, who have the existing laws in their favour; the second is the incredulity common to all men, who do not want to believe in the goodness of new things until they have been well convinced by experience. This is also the reason why, if those who are enemies find an opportunity to attack, they do so with all the heat of partisanship, and the others defend themselves with coldness, so that it is dangerous to fight with them.

In order to reason properly on this subject, we need to consider whether innovators are powerful in their own right, or whether they are dependent on others, i.e. whether they are reduced to praying in order to conduct their business, or whether they have the means to coerce.

In the first case, misfortune always befalls them, and they succeed in nothing; but in the second, on the contrary, that is to say when they depend only on themselves, and are in a position to force, they very rarely run the risk of succumbing. This is why we have seen all the armed prophets succeed, and those who were unarmed unfortunately end. To which we should add that people are naturally fickle, and that while it is easy to persuade them of something, it is difficult to make them firm in that persuasion: things must therefore be arranged in such a way that, when they no longer believe, they can be made to believe by force.

Certainly Moses, Cyrus, Theseus and Romulus would not have been able to keep their institutions for long if they had been unarmed; and they would have suffered the same fate as Friar Jerome Savonarola, whose institutions perished as soon as many began to disbelieve in him, since he had no means of strengthening in their belief those who still believed, or of forcing those who disbelieved to believe.

However, let us repeat that great men such as these encounter extreme difficulties; that all dangers are in their path; that it is there that they have to overcome them; and that once they have overcome these obstacles, once they have begun to be revered, and once they have freed themselves from those of the same rank who were envious of them, they remain powerful, tranquil, honoured and happy.

To these great examples that I have cited, I want to add another of a lesser order, but one that is not too disproportionate; and I choose just one that will suffice: that of Hieron of Syracuse. A simple private citizen, he became prince of his homeland, owing nothing more to fortune than opportunity. Indeed, the oppressed Syracusans elected him as their general, and it was through his services in this capacity that he still deserves to be elevated to supreme power. Moreover, in his first state as a citizen, he had shown so many virtues that it has been said of him that all he needed to reign well was a kingdom. In addition, Hieron destroyed the old militia and established a new one; he abandoned the old alliances to enter into new ones: having then both soldiers and allies entirely his own,

23

he was able, on such foundations, to erect the edifice he wanted; so that, if he acquired only with great difficulty, he found none to keep.

CHAPTER VII. New principalities acquired by the arms of others and by fortune.

Those who go from being mere private individuals to becoming princes by the mere favour of fortune, do so with little difficulty; but they have a great deal of difficulty in maintaining themselves. No difficulty stops them in their tracks: they fly along; but they show themselves when they arrive.

Such were those to whom a state was granted, either for a sum of money or at the pleasure of the grantor. This is how a host of concessions were made in Ionia and on the banks of the Hellespont, where Darius established various princes to govern these states for his safety and glory. This is also how those emperors were created who, from the rank of simple citizens, were raised to the empire by the corruption of soldiers. The existence of such princes depends entirely on two very uncertain and very variable things: the will and the fortune of those who created them; and they neither know nor can maintain their elevation. They cannot, because unless a man is gifted with a great mind and great worth, it is unlikely that, having always lived as a private individual, he will know how to command; they cannot, because they have no forces that are attached to them and loyal to them.

Moreover, States formed suddenly are like all things which, in the order of nature, are born and grow too quickly: they cannot have roots deep enough and adhesions strong enough for the first storm not to topple them; unless, as I have just said, those who have become princes have enough skill to know how to prepare themselves immediately to keep what fortune has placed in their hands, and to found, after the rise of their power, the foundations that should have been established beforehand.

With regard to these two ways of becoming a prince, i.e. by skill or by fortune, I would like to cite two examples that are still remembered today: those of Francesco Sforza and Caesar Borgia.

Francesco Sforza, through great valour and the use of appropriate means alone, went from being a private citizen to Duke of Milan; and what had cost him so much work to acquire, he had little trouble keeping.

On the contrary, Caesar Borgia, commonly known as the Duke of Valentinois, who became a prince through his father's fortune, lost his principality as soon as that same fortune no longer supported him, even though he had done everything that a prudent and skilful man should do to put down deep roots in the states that the arms of others and fortune had given him. It is not impossible, in fact, as I have already said, for an extremely skilful man to lay, after he has risen to power, foundations that he would not have laid before; but such work is always very painful for the architect and dangerous for the edifice.

Moreover, if we examine the Duke's progress carefully, we will see how much he had done to consolidate his future greatness; and this is what it seems worthwhile to dwell on a little; for the example of his actions undoubtedly presents the best lessons that can be given to a new prince, and if all his measures were ultimately unsuccessful for him, it was not through his fault, but through an extraordinary and boundless vexation of fortune.

Alexander VI, wishing to enlarge the dukedom of his son, found many difficulties for the present and for the future. Firstly, he saw that he could only make him master of a State that was in the domain of the Church; and he knew that the Duke of Milan and Venice would not agree to this, especially as Faenza and Rimini were already under the protection of the Venetians. Moreover, he saw that all the forces of Italy, and especially those he could have used, were in the hands of those who were most likely to fear the Pope's expansion; so he could not count on their loyalty, since they were dependent on the Orsini, the Colonna and their supporters. This left him with no option but to confuse everything and sow disorder among all the Italian states, so as to be able to seize some of them through the troubles. This was not difficult. The Venetians had decided, for other reasons, to recall the French to Italy, and not only did he not oppose this plan, but he also facilitated its execution by dissolving the long-standing marriage of King Louis XII to Jeanne de France. This prince therefore came to Italy with the help of the Venetians and the consent of the Pope; and no sooner had he arrived in Milan than Alexander obtained troops for an expedition into the Romagna, which was immediately abandoned to him solely as a result of the king's reputation. Having thus acquired this province, the Duke of Valentinois found his plans to consolidate and make further progress thwarted by two difficulties: one stemmed from the fact that the troops he had did not seem to him to be very loyal; the other had to do with the king's will, that is to say, on the one hand, he feared that the Orsini troops, which he had used, would fail him if necessary, and not only prevent him from making new acquisitions, but would even cause him to lose those he had already made; on the other, he feared that the king would do the same. As for the Orsini troops, he had already had some experience of their dispositions when, after the capture of Faenza, having gone to attack Bologna, he had seen them behave very coldly; and, as for the king, he had been able to read the depths of his thinking when, having wanted, after seizing the duchy of Urbino, to turn his arms against Tuscany, this prince had forced him to withdraw from his undertaking.

In these circumstances, the Duke set about making himself independent of the arms and will of others. To achieve this, he began by weakening the Orsini and Colonna parties in Rome, winning over all their noble adherents, making them his gentlemen, and giving them rich salaries, honours, command of troops and governments of places, according to their status: so it happened that within a few months the affection of all parties turned towards the Duke.

Then, when he had dispersed the supporters of the house of Colonna, he waited for the opportunity to destroy those of the Orsini; and this opportunity having fortunately presented itself to him, he knew how to take advantage of it even more fortunately. Indeed, the Orsini, having recognised a little late that the expansion of the Duke and the Church would be the cause of their ruin, held a kind of diet in a place in the States of Perugia called the Magione; and from this assembly followed the revolt of Urbino, the troubles of Romagna, and an infinite number of dangers that the Duke overcame with the help of the French. Having thereby re-established his reputation, and no longer trusting either France or any other foreign force, he resorted to cunning, and was able to conceal his feelings so well that the Orsini were reconciled with him through the lord Pagolo, whom he had secured by every possible token of friendship, giving him clothes, money and horses. After this reconciliation, they had the simplicity to go and put themselves in his hands at Sinigaglia.

Once these leaders had been destroyed, and their supporters won over by the Duke, he had founded his power all the better, since, moreover, as master of Romagna and the Duchy of Urbino, he had endeared himself to the inhabitants by giving them a taste of well-being. Since his conduct can still serve as an example, it is worth mentioning it here.

Romagna, acquired by the Duke, had previously been ruled by weak men who had robbed rather than governed, divided rather than united their subjects, with the result that the whole country was prey to theft, robbery and violence of every kind. The Duke decided that, in order to restore peace and obedience to the Prince, it was necessary to form a good government: so he appointed Messer Ramiro d'Orco, a cruel and expeditious man, to whom he gave the broadest powers. Soon, in fact, this government brought order and tranquillity, and acquired a very high reputation as a result. But then the duke, thinking that such authority was no longer necessary, and that it might even become odious, established a civil court at the centre of the province, to which he gave a very good president, and where each commune had its own lawyer. He did much more: knowing that the harshness he initially applied had aroused some hatred, and wishing to extinguish this feeling in people's hearts so that they would be entirely devoted to him, he wanted to show that if any cruelties had been committed, they had come, not from him, but from the wickedness of his minister. Seizing the opportunity, he had him exposed one morning in the public square of Caesene, cut into quarters, with a block and a bloody cutlass beside him. This horrible sight satisfied the resentment of the inhabitants and struck them with terror at the same time. But let's come back.

Having given himself the forces he wanted and having largely destroyed those of his neighbours who could harm him, the Duke, finding himself very powerful, believed himself almost entirely secure against the present dangers; and wishing to pursue his conquests, he was still held back by the consideration of France: for he knew that the King, who had finally realised his error, would not allow him to undertake such ventures. Consequently, he began to seek new friendships and to prevaricate with the French, when they marched towards the kingdom of Naples against the

Spaniards, who were laying siege to Gaëte; he even planned to put them in no position to thwart him; and he would soon have succeeded, had Alexander lived longer.

Such were his measures with regard to the present state of affairs. For the future, he first had to fear that a new pope would be ill-disposed towards him and would seek to take away what Alexander, his father, had given him. He wanted to prevent this by the following four means: firstly, by completely extinguishing the races of the lords he had dispossessed, and thus not leaving the pope the opportunities that the existence of these races would have provided him with; secondly, by winning over the gentlemen of Rome, in order to hold the pontiff in respect through them; thirdly, by attaching himself, as far as he could, to the sacred college; fourthly, by making himself, before the death of the pope who was then alive, powerful enough to be in a position to resist by himself a first shock. By the time Alexander died, three of these things had been achieved, and he regarded the fourth as more or less complete. He had effectively killed all the stripped lords he had been able to reach, and very few of them had escaped him; he had won over the Roman gentlemen; he had made himself a very large party in the sacred college; and finally, as for increasing his power, he planned to make himself master of Tuscany : which seemed easy to him, since he was already master of Perugia and Piombino, and he had taken under his protection the city of Pisa, on which he was going to throw himself, without being held back by the consideration of France, which no longer imposed itself on him; for already the French had been stripped of the kingdom of Naples by the Spaniards; so that all parties found themselves in the necessity of seeking the friendship of the Duke. After that, Lucca and Siena would have to submit immediately, either out of fear or envy of the Florentines, who would then be left without resources. If he had carried out this entire plan (and he would have done so in the course of the year in which the Pope died), he would have found himself strong enough and reputable enough to support himself and depend solely on his own power and worth. But Alexander's death occurred when the duke had been sworn in for only five years, and at that moment he found himself with only the State of Romagna well established: in all the others, his power was still wavering; he was placed between two enemy armies and was attacked by a fatal illness.

However, he was gifted with such determination and great courage, he knew so well the art of winning men and destroying them, and the foundations he had laid for his power were so solid that if he had not had two armies on his back, or if he had not been ill, he would have overcome all the difficulties. And what proves the solidity of the foundations he had laid is that the Romagna waited more than a month to decide against him; it is that, although half dead, he remained safe in Rome, and that the Baglioni, the Vitelli and the Orsini, who had rushed to the city, were unable to form a party against him; it is that he was able, if not to have anyone he wanted appointed pope, at least to prevent anyone he did not want from being appointed. If his health had not suffered at the time of Alexander's death, everything would have been easy for him. He also told me, at the time of the appointment of Julius II, that he had thought of everything that could happen if his father died, and that he had found a remedy for everything; but only that he had never imagined that at that moment he himself would be in danger of death.

Summing up the Duke's conduct, not only do I find nothing to criticise in it, but it seems to me that it can be proposed as a model to all those who have attained sovereign power through the favour of fortune and the arms of others. Gifted with great courage and ambition, he could not have behaved otherwise; and the execution of his plans could only be halted by the brevity of his father Alexander's life and by his own illness. Whoever, in a new principality, deems it necessary to secure himself against his enemies, to make friends, to win by force or by cunning, to make himself loved and feared by the people, followed and respected by the soldiers, to destroy those who can and must harm him, to replace the old institutions with new ones, to be both severe and gracious, magnanimous and liberal, to form a new militia and dissolve the old one, to spare the friendship of kings and princes, in such a way that all must love to oblige him and fear to do him injustice : he, I say, cannot find more recent examples than those found in the political life of the Duc de Valentinois.

The only thing we have to criticise in his conduct is the appointment of Julius II, which was a disastrous choice for him. Since he could not, as I have said, have anyone he wanted elected pope, but prevent anyone he did not want from being elected, he should never have consented to the elevation to the papacy of one of the cardinals he had offended, and who, having become Supreme Pontiff, would have had reason to fear him; for resentment and fear are above all what make men enemies.

Those whom the Duke had offended were, among others, the Cardinals of Saint-Pierre ès liens, Colonna, Saint-Georges and Ascanio Sforza; and all the others had reason to fear him, except the Cardinal d'Amboise, and the Spaniards: the latter, because of certain reciprocal relations and obligations, and d'Amboise, because he had France to himself, which gave him great power. The Duke therefore preferred to have a Spaniard appointed, and if he could not, to consent to the election of d'Amboise rather than that of Cardinal de Saint-Pierre ès liens. It is a mistake to imagine that, in the case of great people, recent services make one forget old insults. The Duke, in consenting to this election by Julius II, therefore made a mistake which was the cause of his total ruin.

CHAPTER VIII. Of those who have become princes by scoundrels.

There are two other ways of becoming a prince which do not depend entirely on fortune or worth, and which should not therefore be overlooked; there is even one which could be discussed at greater length if we were dealing here with republics.

These two ways are either to rise to sovereign power by villainy and crime, or to be brought to it by the favour of his fellow citizens.

To illustrate the first, which I do not intend to examine here from the point of view of justice and morality, I shall limit myself to citing two examples, one ancient, the other modern; for it seems to me that they may suffice for anyone who finds it necessary to imitate them.

Agathocles, a Sicilian, rose not only from the rank of a private citizen, but from the most abject state to become King of Syracuse. The son of a potter, he showed himself to be a villain at every stage of his fortune, but he combined his villainy with such strength of mind and body that, having embarked on a military career, he rose from rank to the dignity of praetor of Syracuse. Having reached this elevation, he wanted to be a prince, and even to possess by violence, and without being obliged to anyone, the sovereign power that he had been granted. To achieve this aim, having consulted with Amilcar, a Carthaginian general commanding an army in Sicily, he summoned the people and senate of Syracuse one morning, as if to deliberate on matters concerning the republic; at a given signal, he had his soldiers massacre all the senators and the richest citizens, after which he seized the principality, which he retained without any dispute. Afterwards, beaten twice by the Carthaginians and finally besieged by them in Syracuse, he was not only able to defend it, but also, leaving part of his troops to support the siege, he went with the other to carry the war to Africa; so that in a short time he was able to force the Carthaginians to lift the siege and reduce them to the last extremities: So they were forced to make peace with him, to relinquish possession of Sicily to him, and to content themselves with that of Africa.

Anyone who reflects on Agathocles' career and actions will find little, if anything, that can be attributed to fortune. In fact, as I have just said, he rose to supreme power, not through favour, but by passing through all the military ranks, which he gained successively by dint of hard work and danger; and when he had attained this power, he knew how to hold on to it by the boldest and most perilous resolutions.

Truly, it cannot be said that there is any value in massacring one's fellow citizens, betraying one's friends, being without faith, without pity, without religion: one can acquire power by such means, but not glory. But if we consider the courage with which Agathocles rushed into and out of danger, the fortitude with which he suffered and overcame adversity, we see no reason why he should be placed below the best captains. We can only admit that his cruelty, his inhumanity and his many scoundrels do not allow us to count him among the great men. Let us therefore confine ourselves to concluding that neither fortune nor virtue can be credited with the elevation he achieved without both.

In our time, during the reign of Alexander VI, Oliverotto da Fermo, who had been orphaned in infancy several years earlier, was brought up by a maternal uncle named John Fogliani, and from his earliest youth was trained in the profession of arms under the discipline of Paolo Vitelli, so that, trained in such a good school, he could attain a high military rank. After Paolo's death, he continued to serve under Vitelozzo, the brother of his first master. Soon, thanks to his talent, physical strength and intrepid courage, he became one of the most distinguished officers in the army. But as it seemed to him that there was servility in being under the orders and in the pay of others, he formed the project of making himself master of Fermo, both with the help of some citizens who preferred slavery to the freedom of their homeland, and with the support of Vitelozzo. With this in mind, he wrote to John Fogliani that, having been away from himself and his homeland for many years, he wanted to go and see them again, and at the same time see a little of his heritage; that, moreover, since all his work had only honour as its object, and since he wanted his fellow citizens to see that he had not spent his time in vain, he proposed to go and show himself to them with a certain amount of pomp, accompanied by a hundred of his friends and servants on horseback; that he would therefore ask him to arrange for the people of Fermo to give him an honourable reception, as this would not only bring glory to himself but also to his uncle, whose pupil he was. Jean Fogliani did everything he could to oblige his nephew. He had him received honourably by the inhabitants; he put him up in his house, where, after a few days spent making the necessary preparations for the accomplishment of his crimes, Oliverotto gave a magnificent feast, to which he invited both John Fogliani and the most distinguished citizens of Fermo. After all the services and entertainment that take place at such feasts, he skilfully turned the conversation to serious subjects, speaking of the greatness of Pope Alexander and his son Caesar, as well as their undertakings. John Fogliani and the others having expressed their opinion on this subject, he suddenly rose, saying that these were matters to be dealt with in a more secluded place; and he passed into another room, where the guests followed him. But no sooner were they seated than soldiers came out of various secret places and killed them all, along with John Fogliani. Immediately after this murder, Oliverotto mounted his horse, rode through the country and went to besiege the supreme magistrate in his palace, so that fear forced everyone to obey him and form a government of which he made himself the prince. Moreover, all those who might have harmed him through their discontent having been put to death, he consolidated his power with new civil and military institutions to such an extent that, in the course of the year during which he held it, he not only lived in safety at home, but also made himself formidable to his neighbours; And he would have been no less difficult to defeat than Agathocles, had he not allowed himself to be deceived by Caesar Borgia, and lured to Sinigaglia, where, a year after the parricide he had committed, he was taken with the Orsini and the Vitelli, as I said above, and strangled, along with Vitelozzo, his master of war and villainy.

Someone may ask why Agathocles, or some other similar tyrant, was able, in spite of an infinite number of treacheries and cruelties, to live for a long time in safety in his homeland, to defend himself against his external enemies, and not to have to fight any conspiracy formed by his fellow citizens; whereas many others, for having been cruel, were unable to maintain themselves either in times of war or in times of peace. I believe that the reason for this lies in the use or misuse of cruelty. Cruelties are well used (if, however, the word well can ever be applied to what is evil) when they are committed all at once, out of the need to provide for one's own safety, when one does not persist in doing so, and when one turns them, as far as possible, to the advantage of one's subjects. They are misused, on the other hand, when, though few in number in principle, they multiply with time instead of ceasing.

Those who use it well can, like Agathocles, with the help of God and men, remedy the consequences; but for those who use it badly, it is impossible to maintain themselves.

On this point, it should be observed that he who usurps a State must determine and carry out all the cruelties he is to commit at once, so that he does not have to return to them every day, and so that he can, by avoiding repeating them, reassure the spirits and win them over with benefits. He who, through timidity or bad advice, behaves otherwise, finds himself obliged to always have the sword in his hand, and he can never count on his subjects, who are constantly worried by constant and recent insults. Cruelties must be committed all at once, so that their bitterness is felt less and they irritate less; benefits, on the other hand, must follow one another slowly, so that they are savoured more.

In all matters, the prince must behave towards his subjects in such a way that he is not seen to vary according to good or bad circumstances. If he waits until he is forced by necessity to do evil or good, it will happen either that he will no longer be in time to do evil, or that the good he does will not benefit him at all; for it will be thought that he did it by force, and he will not be thanked for it.

CHAPTER IX. The civil principality.

Let us now turn to the individual who has become a prince of his country, not through villainy or atrocious violence, but through the favour of his fellow citizens: this is what may be called a civil principality, which is achieved not by skill or virtue alone, but rather by skill.

In this respect, I would say that one is elevated to this kind of principality either by the favour of the people or by that of the great. In all countries, in fact, there are two opposing attitudes: on the one hand, the people do not want to be commanded or oppressed by the great; on the other, the great wish to command and oppress the people; and these opposing attitudes produce one of three effects: principality, liberty or licence.

The principality can also be the work either of the great or of the people, depending on the occasion. When the great ones see that they cannot resist the people, they turn to the credit and ascendancy of one of them and make him a prince so that, under the shadow of his authority, they can satisfy their ambitious desires; similarly, when the people cannot resist the great ones, they put all their trust in an individual and make him a prince so that they can be defended by his power.

The prince raised by the great has more difficulty maintaining his position than one who owes his elevation to the people. The former, in fact, finds himself surrounded by men who believe themselves to be his equals, and whom he can therefore neither command nor manage as he pleases; the latter, on the other hand, finds himself alone in his position, and he has no one around him, or almost no one, who is not prepared to obey him. Moreover, it is scarcely possible to please the great without some injustice, without some insult to others; but the same cannot be said of the people, whose aim is more equitable than that of the great. The latter want to oppress, and the people only want not to be oppressed. It is true that if the people become enemies, the prince cannot be sure of it, because the multitude is too great; whereas, on the contrary, it is very easy for him with regard to the nobles, who are always few in number. But, in the worst case, all he can fear from the people is to be abandoned by them, whereas he must still fear that the great ones will act against him; for, having more foresight and skill, they always know how to provide themselves with means of salvation from afar, and they seek to gain favour with the party in which they expect victory to remain. Let us observe, moreover, that the people with whom the prince must live are always the same, and that he cannot change them; but that, as for the great ones, change is easy; that he can make or break them every day; that he can, as he pleases, either increase or decrease their credit: on which it may be useful to give some clarifications here.

I therefore say that, in relation to the great, there is a first and principal distinction to be made between those whose conduct shows that they attach their fortune entirely to that of the prince, and those who act differently.

The former are to be honoured and cherished, provided they are not inclined to plunder: as for the others, a further distinction must be made. If there are those who act in this way through weakness and a natural lack of courage, they may be employed, especially if, moreover, they are men of good counsel, because the prince is honoured by them in prosperous times and has nothing to fear from them in adversity. But for those who know well what they are doing, and who are determined by ambitious views, it is obvious that they are thinking of themselves rather than of the prince. He must therefore distrust them and regard them as if they were his declared enemies; for, in the event of adversity, they will infallibly help to bring about his ruin.

To conclude, here is the consequence of all that has just been said. He who becomes a prince through the favour of the people must work to keep their friendship, which is easy, since the people ask for nothing more than not to be oppressed. As for the person who becomes a prince through the favour of the nobles, against the will of the people, he must first of all try to win them over, and this is easy too, since all he has to do is take them under his protection. Even then the people will become more submissive and more devoted to him than if the principality had been obtained through his favour; for when men receive some good from him from whom they expected only evil, they are much more grateful. I will only repeat that it is absolutely necessary for a prince to have the friendship of his people, and that if he does not have it, he lacks all resources in adversity.

Nabis, Prince of Sparta, was besieged by the whole of Greece and by a Roman army which had already won several victories, so that he could resist and defend his homeland and his power against such forces. In such great danger, he only had to rely on a very small number of people, which would undoubtedly have been far from enough if he had had the enmity of the people against him.

Let no one object to the common proverb: He who relies on the people relies on the mud. This is true for an individual who relies on such a foundation, and who believes that if he is oppressed by his enemies or by magistrates, the people will embrace his defence; his hope will often be disappointed, as was the hope of the Gracchi in Rome and of Messer Giorgio Scali in Florence. However, if the prince in question has the right to command, is a man of heart, is not discouraged in adversity, has not failed to take other appropriate measures, and knows how to dominate his subjects through his firmness, he will not be disappointed, and he will see that by relying on the people he has built his position on a very solid foundation.

The princes in question are only really in danger when they want to turn civil power into absolute power, either by exercising it themselves or through magistrates. But in the latter case, they are weaker and in greater danger, because they depend on the will of the citizens to whom the magistracies are entrusted, and who, especially in times of adversity, can very easily destroy the authority of the prince, either by acting against him or simply by not obeying him. In vain would this prince then wish to resume the exercise of his power for himself alone, it would no longer be the time, because the citizens and subjects, accustomed to receiving orders from the mouths of magistrates, would not be prepared, in critical moments, to obey those he would give himself. So, in these uncertain times, he will always find it very difficult to find friends in whom he can confide.

Such a prince should not regulate what happens in times of tranquillity and when the citizens need his authority: But in times of adversity, when he needs all the citizens, he will find very few who are willing to defend him: this is what experience would show him; but this experience is all the more dangerous to attempt because it can only be done once. The prince must therefore, if he is endowed with any wisdom, devise and establish a system of government such that at any time, and in spite of all circumstances, the citizens will need him: then he will always be sure to find them loyal.

CHAPTER X. How, in any kind of principality, one must measure one's forces.

In speaking of the various kinds of principalities, there is yet another thing to consider: whether the prince has a State powerful enough to be able, if necessary, to defend itself by itself, or whether it is always necessary for him to be defended by another.

To make my thinking clearer, I consider princes who have enough men and enough money at their disposal to form a complete army and fight anyone who comes to attack them to be capable of defending themselves; on the other hand, I consider those who do not have the means to start a campaign against the enemy, and who are obliged to take refuge within their walls and defend themselves there, to be always in need of help from others.

I've already spoken about the former, and in what follows I'll say a few more words about what will happen to the latter.

As for the others, all I can say to them is to exhort them to provide well, to fortify well the city where the seat of their power is established, and to take no account of the rest of the country. Whenever a prince has vigorously provided for the defence of his capital and has won the affection of his subjects through the other acts of his government, as I have said and will say again, he should only be attacked with great circumspection; for men in general do not like undertakings that present great difficulties; and there are undoubtedly many who would attack a prince whose city is in a respectable state of defence and who is not hated by his subjects.

The cities of Germany enjoy a great deal of freedom, even though they possess only a very small territory; however, they obey the emperor only as much as they please, and fear neither his power nor that of any of the other states around them: they are fortified in such a way that a siege of them would be a difficult and dangerous operation; they are all surrounded by ditches and good walls, and they have sufficient artillery; they always have a year's supply of food, drink and fuel in the public shops; They even have enough materials to sustain the common people, without any loss to the public, to provide them with work for a whole year in the type of industry and trade they usually engage in, and which makes up the wealth and life of the country; moreover, they keep military exercises in honour, and have a large number of regulations on this subject.

So a prince whose city is well fortified, and who is not hated by his subjects, must not fear being attacked; and if he were, the attacker would turn back in shame: for the things of this world are changeable; and it is hardly possible for an enemy to remain encamped with his troops around a place for a whole year.

If it were objected to me that the inhabitants who have their properties outside would not see them handed over to the flames with an untroubled eye; that the boredom of the siege and their personal interests would not let them think much about the prince, I would reply that a powerful and courageous prince will always be able to overcome these difficulties, either by making his subjects hope that the evil will not be long-lasting, or by making them fear the cruelty of the enemy, or by prudently assuring himself of those whom he would judge too bold.

Moreover, if the enemy burns and ravages the country, it must naturally be at the moment of his arrival, that is to say at a time when spirits are still all fired up and ready to defend: the prince should therefore be all the less alarmed in this circumstance, since when these same spirits have begun to cool, it will be found that the damage has already been done and suffered, that there is no longer any remedy, and that the inhabitants will only become more attached to their prince, by the thought that he owes them a debt of gratitude for the fact that their houses have been set on fire and their countryside ravaged in his defence. Such is the nature of men, in fact, that they become attached as much by the services they render as by those they receive. So, all things considered, it should not be difficult for a prudent prince, besieged in his city, to inspire firmness in the inhabitants, and to maintain them in this attitude as long as they have the means to feed and defend themselves.

CHAPTER XI. Ecclesiastical Principalities.

It now remains to speak of ecclesiastical principalities, in relation to which there is no difficulty except in obtaining possession. Indeed, they are acquired either by the favour of fortune or by the ascendancy of virtue; but afterwards, in order to keep them, one needs neither the one nor the other: for the princes are supported by the ancient religious institutions, whose power is so great and whose nature is such that they maintain them in power, in whatever way they govern and conduct themselves.

These princes alone have states, and they do not defend them; they have subjects, and they do not govern them. Yet their states, though undefended, are not taken away from them; and their subjects, though ungoverned, are not troubled by them, nor do they wish to or can they detach themselves from them. These principalities are therefore free from peril and happy. But since this is due to higher causes, to which the human mind cannot rise, I will not speak of them. It is God who raises them up and maintains them, and any man who undertakes to discuss them would be guilty of presumption and temerity.

However, if anyone asks why the Church has risen to such temporal greatness, and why, before Alexander VI and up to him, all those who had any power in Italy, and not only the princes but also the least barons and the least lords, feared her power so little in the temporal sphere, she has now come to make the King of France tremble, to drive him out of Italy and to ruin the Venetians; Although everyone is aware of this, it does not seem pointless to recall it here to some extent.

Before Charles VIII, King of France, came to Italy, the country was under the domination of the Pope, the Venetians, the King of Naples, the Duke of Milan and the Florentines. Each of these powers had two main concerns: one was to prevent any foreigners from bringing their arms into Italy; the other was to prevent any of them from enlarging their states. As for this second point, it was above all the Pope and the Venetians that needed to be watched. To contain the latter, all the other powers had to remain united, as happened during the defence of Ferrara; and, as far as the Pope was concerned, the barons of Rome were used, who, divided into two factions, that of the Orsini and that of the Colonna, continually stirred up tumults, always had their weapons in their hands under the very eyes of the pontiff, and constantly kept his power weak and wavering. From time to time, there were a few resolute and courageous popes, such as Sixtus IV, but they were never skilful or fortunate enough to free themselves from the unfortunate embarrassments they had to suffer. Moreover, they found a new obstacle in the brevity of their reigns: for, in an interval of ten years, which is the average length of the reigns of popes, it was hardly possible to completely bring down one of the factions that divided Rome; and if, for example, one pope had brought down the Colonna, another pope would come along and revive them, because he was an enemy of the Orsini; but this pope, in turn, did not have the time needed to destroy the Orsini. This is why Italy had so little respect for the Pope's temporal power.

Finally came Alexander VI, who, of all the pontiffs who have ever lived, is the one who has best shown what a pope could do to increase his power with the treasures and arms of the Church. Taking advantage of the invasion of the French, and making use of an instrument such as the Duke of Valentinois, he did all that I have described above when speaking of the latter's actions. His aim was undoubtedly not the enlargement of the Church, but that of the Duke; nevertheless, his endeavours benefited the Church, which, after his death and the Duke's ruin, inherited the fruits of their labours.

Soon afterwards reigned Julius II, who, finding that the Church was powerful and master of all Romagna; that the barons had been destroyed, and their factions annihilated by the rigours of Alexander; he not only wanted to follow in these footsteps, but also to go further, and set about acquiring Bologna, destroying the Venetians, and driving the French out of Italy; undertakings in which he succeeded with all the more glory, since he had undertaken them, not for his personal interest, but for that of the Church.

Moreover, he was able to contain the parties of the Colonna and Orsini within the limits which Alexander had managed to reduce them to; and, although there were still some seeds of discord between them, they nevertheless had to remain calm, firstly because the greatness of the

Church imposed upon them; and, secondly, because they had no cardinals among them. It is the cardinals, in fact, who must be blamed for the tumults, and the parties will never be calm as long as the cardinals are involved: it is they who foment the factions, whether in Rome or outside, and who force the barons to support them; so that the dissensions and disturbances that break out among the barons are the work of the ambition of the prelates.

This, then, is how Pope Leo X came to find the Papacy all-powerful; and it is to be hoped that if his predecessors enlarged it by their arms, he will make it even greater and more venerable by his goodness and all his other virtues.

CHAPTER XII. How many kinds of militia and mercenary troops there are.

I have spoken of the qualities peculiar to the various kinds of principalities which I proposed to discuss; I have examined some of the causes of their evil or their well-being; I have shown the means which many have used, either to acquire them or to keep them: it now remains for me to consider them from the point of view of attack and defence.

I said above how necessary it is for a prince that his power be established on good foundations, without which it cannot fail to collapse. Now, for any state, whether old, new or mixed, the main foundations are good laws and good weapons. But, since where there are no good weapons, there can be no good laws, and since on the contrary there are good laws where there are good weapons, it is only about weapons that I intend to speak here.

I therefore say that the weapons that a prince can use for the defence of his State are his own, or are mercenary, auxiliary or mixed, and that mercenaries and auxiliaries are not only useless, but even dangerous.

A prince whose power is supported only by mercenary troops will never be secure or at peace; for such troops are disunited, ambitious, undisciplined, unfaithful, bold towards friends, cowardly against enemies; and they have neither fear of God nor probity towards men. It will only be a matter of time before the prince is ruined insofar as we delay attacking him. During peacetime, he will be robbed by these same troops; during wartime, he will be robbed by the enemy.

The reason for this is that such soldiers serve without any affection, and are only obliged to bear arms for a small salary; a motive that is no doubt incapable of determining them to die for the person who employs them. They are willing to be soldiers as long as there is no war, but as soon as it comes they know only how to run away and desert.

This is what I should have little difficulty in persuading. It is clear, in fact, that the present ruin of Italy is due to the fact that, over a long period of years, it has relied on mercenary troops, which some had initially employed with some success, and which had seemed valorous as long as they had only had to deal with each other, but which, as soon as a foreigner arrived, showed themselves to be what they really were. From this it follows that Charles VIII, King of France, was able to seize Italy with chalk in his hand[5]; and he who said that our sins were the cause was right; but these sins were those I have just described, not those he thought. These sins, moreover, had been committed by the princes, and it was they too who suffered the penalty.

However, I want to demonstrate more and more the misfortune attached to this kind of weapon. Mercenary captains are either good warriors or they are not: if they are, they cannot be trusted, because they tend only to their own greatness, oppressing either the prince who employs them or others against his will; if they are not, the one they serve is soon ruined.

If it is said that this would also be the conduct of any other leader, whether mercenary or not, I would reply that war is waged either by a prince or by a republic; that the prince must go in person to perform the duties of commander; and that the republic must send its own citizens: that if at first the one it has chosen does not show himself to be skilful, it must change him; and that if he is skilful it must restrain him by the laws, in such a way that he does not overstep the bounds of his commission.

Experience has shown that princes and republics who wage war with their own forces alone achieve great success, and that mercenary troops never cause anything but harm. It also proves that a republic that uses its own weapons runs far less risk of being subjugated by one of its citizens than one that uses foreign weapons.

For many centuries Rome and Sparta were free and armed; Switzerland, whose inhabitants are all soldiers, is perfectly free.

As for mercenary troops, we can cite the ancient example of the Carthaginians, who, after their first war against Rome, were on the point of being oppressed by the troops they had in their service, even though they were commanded by citizens of Carthage.

It should also be noted that after the death of Epaminondas, the Thebans entrusted the command of their troops to Philip of Macedonia, and that this prince used the victory to rob them of their freedom.

In modern times, the Milanese, on the death of their duke Philip Visconti, were at war with the Venetians; they took Francesco Sforza into their pay: having defeated the enemies at Carravaggio, he joined forces with them to oppress the same Milanese who had taken him into their pay.

The father of this same Sforza, being in the service of Queen Joan of Naples, had suddenly left her without troops, so that, in order not to lose her kingdom, this princess had been obliged to throw herself into the arms of the king of Aragon.

If the Venetians and Florentines, by employing such troops, nonetheless increased their States, and if the commanders, instead of subjugating them, defended them, I reply, as far as the Florentines are concerned, that they were indebted to their good fortune, which meant that, of all the skilful generals they had and could fear, some were not victorious; others encountered obstacles; still others turned their ambitions elsewhere.

One of the first was Giovanni Acuto, whose loyalty, by the very fact that he had not won, was not put to the test; but it must be admitted that, had he won, the Florentines would have remained at his discretion.

Sforza was annoyed by the Braccios' rivalry, which meant that they kept each other in check.

Finally, Francesco Sforza and Braccio turned their ambitious sights, one on Lombardy, the other on the Church and the Kingdom of Naples.

But let's look at what happened a short while ago.

The Florentines had chosen Paolo Vitelli as their general, a man of great ability who had risen from the position of a private to a very high reputation. Now, if this general had succeeded in making himself master of Pisa, we are forced to admit that they would have found themselves under his dependence; for if he passed over to the pay of their enemies, they had no resources left; and if they continued to keep him in their service, they were forced to submit to his wishes.

As for the Venetians, if we consider their progress carefully, we will see that they acted happily and gloriously as long as they waged war on their own, in other words before they had turned their ventures towards dry land. In those early days, it was the gentlemen and armed citizens who fought; but as soon as they began to carry their weapons on dry land, they degenerated from this ancient virtue and followed the customs of Italy. At first, and in the principle of their expansion, their domain being small and their reputation very great, they had little to fear from their commanders; but, as their state grew, they soon experienced the effect of the common error: this was under Carmignuola. Having become aware of his great valour through the victories he had won under his command over the Duke of Milan, but seeing, on the other hand, that he now only waged war very coldly, they judged that they could no longer win as long as he lived; for they were neither willing nor able to dismiss him for fear of losing what they had conquered; and consequently they were obliged, for their own safety, to have him killed.

Later, they were commanded by Bartolommeo of Bergamo, Roberto da San Severino, the Count of Pittigliano and other similar captains. But all of them gave far less cause to fear their victories than defeats similar to that of Vailà, which in a single day caused the Venetians to lose the fruit of eight hundred years' work; for, with the troops in question, progress is slow, late and feeble, while losses are sudden and prodigious.

But, since I have come to cite examples taken from Italy, where the system of mercenary troops has prevailed for many years, I want to start again at a higher level, so that, informed of the origin and progress of this system, we can better remedy it.

It should be noted, therefore, that when the empire began to be pushed out of Italy in recent times, and the pope gained more credit in temporal matters, it was divided into a large number of states. Several large cities took up arms against their nobles, who were oppressing them under the shadow of imperial authority, and made themselves independent, a move favoured by the Church, which sought to increase the credit it had won. In several other cities, supreme power was usurped or obtained by some citizen who established himself as prince. As a result, most of Italy found itself under the dependence and, in a way, under the domination of the

Church or of some republic; and as priests, peaceful citizens, had no knowledge of the use of arms, they began to pay foreigners. The first to introduce this type of militia was Alberigo da Como, a native of Romagna: It was under his discipline that, among others, Braccio and Sforza were formed, who were, in their time, the arbiters of Italy, and after them came successively all those who, up to the present day, have held in their hands the command of its armies; and all the fruit that this unfortunate region has reaped from the valour of all these warriors, has been to see itself taken on the run by Charles VIII, ravaged by Louis XII, subjugated by Ferdinand, and insulted by the Swiss.

The course they followed to establish their reputation was to disparage the infantry. On the one hand, a small number of infantrymen would not have earned them much respect, and on the other, since they had no state and subsisted solely on their industry, they did not have the means to maintain many of them. They therefore confined themselves to cavalry, a mediocre quantity of which was sufficient for them to be well paid and honoured: as a result, things had come to the point where, out of an army of twenty thousand men, there were not two thousand infantry.

Moreover, they employed all sorts of means to spare themselves and their soldiers any fatigue or danger: They did not kill each other in battle, and confined themselves to taking prisoners whom they sent back without ransom; if they laid siege to a place, they did not make any night attacks; and the besieged, for their part, did not take advantage of the darkness to make sorties: they did not build ditches or palisades around their camp; finally, they never held the field during the winter. All this was in keeping with their military discipline, an order they had devised on purpose to avoid peril and hard labour, but which they also used to lead Italy into slavery and degradation[6].

CHAPTER XIII. Auxiliary, mixed and clean troops.

Auxiliary arms, which we have said are equally useless, are those of a powerful state that another state calls upon for help and defence. Thus, in recent times, Pope Julius II, having made the sad experience of mercenary arms in his undertaking against Ferrara, had recourse to auxiliaries and negotiated with Ferdinand, King of Spain, for the latter to help him with his troops.

Weapons of this kind may be good in themselves, but they are always harmful to the one who calls on them; for if they are defeated, he himself is defeated, and if they are victorious, he remains dependent on them.

There are many examples of this in ancient history, but let's look for a moment at the recent case of Julius II.

It was undoubtedly an ill-considered decision on his part to surrender to a foreigner in order to take Ferrara. If he did not suffer all the disastrous consequences, he was indebted to his lucky star, which preserved him from them by an accident that it brought about: his auxiliaries were defeated at Ravenna, and then the Swiss arrived, who, against all expectations, drove out the victors; so that he remained a prisoner neither of the latter, who were his enemies, nor of his auxiliaries, who finally found themselves victorious only through the arms of others.

The Florentines, finding themselves unarmed, took ten thousand Frenchmen into their pay and led them to Pisa, which they wanted to take control of, thereby exposing themselves to greater danger than they had faced during their greatest adversities.

To resist his enemies, the emperor of Constantinople introduced ten thousand Turks into Greece, who, when the war was over, would not withdraw: it was this disastrous measure that began to bend the Greeks under the yoke of the infidels.

If you want to make yourself powerless to win, employ auxiliary troops, who are even more dangerous than mercenaries. With the former, in fact, your ruin is all set; for these troops are all united and all trained to obey someone other than you; whereas, as for the mercenaries, for them to be able to act against you, and to harm you after having conquered, they need both more time and a more favourable opportunity: they do not form a single body; it is you who have assembled them, it is you who pays them. Whatever leader you have given them, it is not possible for him to immediately take such authority over them that he can use it against you. In short, what we must fear from mercenary troops is their cowardice; with auxiliary troops, it is their valour. This is why wise princes have always been reluctant to employ these two kinds of troops, preferring their own forces, preferring to be defeated with them than victorious with those of others, and not considering as a real victory that for which they may be indebted to foreign forces.

I have no hesitation in quoting Caesar Borgia and his way of acting. This Duke entered Romagna with auxiliary forces composed entirely of French troops, with which he took Imola and Forli; but soon judging that such forces were not very secure, he resorted to mercenaries, in whom he saw less danger; and, consequently, he took the Orsini and the Vitelli into his pay. However, when he employed them, he found that they were uncertain, unfaithful and dangerous, so he decided to destroy them and use only his own forces.

The difference between these different types of weapons was clearly demonstrated by the difference between the reputation the Duke had when he used the Orsini and the Vitelli, and the reputation he enjoyed when he relied solely on himself and his own soldiers: this reputation grew steadily, and he was never more highly regarded than when everyone saw him as the absolute master of his weapons.

I wanted to confine myself to the recent examples provided by Italy, but I cannot pass over in silence that of Hieron of Syracuse, of whom I have already spoken. When the Syracusans put him at the head of their army, he soon realised the uselessness of the mercenary troops they were paying, whose leaders resembled in every way the condottieri we had in Italy. Convinced, moreover, that he could surely neither keep these leaders nor dismiss them, he took the decision to have them cut to pieces; afterwards, he waged war with his own weapons and not with those of others.

Allow me to recall here a story found in the Old Testament, which may be regarded as a figure of speech on this subject. When David offered to go and fight the Philistine Goliath, who was defying the Israelites, Saul, in order to encourage him, clothed him in his own weapons; but David, after trying them out, refused them, saying that they would hinder the use of his personal strength, and that he wanted to face the enemy only with his slingshot and cutlass. Indeed, other people's weapons are either too large to fit your body properly, or they tire it out with their weight, or they squeeze it and hinder its movements.

Charles VII, father of Louis XI, having delivered France from the English through his wealth and valour, recognised the need for his own forces and formed regular companies of gendarmes and infantrymen in his kingdom. Subsequently, Louis, his son, abolished the infantry and began to take the Swiss into his pay; but this mistake, which led to others, was the cause, as we see, of the dangers faced by France. In fact, by giving pride of place to the Swiss, Louis in a way destroyed all his own troops: firstly, he totally destroyed the infantry; and as for the gendarmerie, he made it dependent on the weapons of others, by accustoming it so much to fighting only in conjunction with the Swiss that it no longer believed it could win without them. This also means that the French cannot stand against the Swiss, and that without the Swiss they cannot stand against other troops. Thus the French armies are currently mixed, that is to say composed partly of mercenary troops and partly of national troops; a composition which undoubtedly makes them much better than armies formed entirely of mercenaries or auxiliaries, but very much inferior to those in which there would only be national corps.

If the order established by Charles VII had been preserved and improved, France would have become invincible. But weak human prudence allows itself to be seduced by the apparent goodness which, in many things, covers up the venom they contain, and which is only recognised later, as in those fevers of étisie of which I spoke earlier. However, the prince who only knows how to see evil when it is plain for all to see is not gifted with this ability, which is given to only a small number of men.

If we look for the main source of the ruin of the Roman Empire, we will find it in the introduction of the practice of taking Goths into one's pay: in effect, this began to weaken the national troops, so that all the value they lost turned to the advantage of the barbarians.

I therefore conclude that no prince is safe unless he has forces of his own: finding himself defenceless against adversity, his fate depends entirely on fortune. Now enlightened men have always thought and said that there is nothing so frail and so fleeting as a credit that is not founded on our own power.

I call, moreover, own forces, those which are composed of citizens, subjects, creatures of the prince. All the others are either mercenaries or auxiliaries.

And as for the means and the way to have these forces of one's own, one will easily find them, if one reflects on the establishments of which I have had occasion to speak. We will see how Philip, father of Alexander the Great, and a host of other princes and republics, were able to create and organise national troops. I refer to the instruction that can be drawn from these examples.

CHAPTER XIV. The functions of the prince in relation to the militia.

This is the true profession of anyone who governs; and through it, not only those who are born princes can maintain themselves, but also those who are born simple private citizens can often become princes. It is because they have neglected arms and preferred the pleasures of softness that we have seen sovereigns lose their States. To despise the art of war is to take the first step towards ruin; to possess it perfectly is the means to rise to power. It was through the constant handling of arms that Francesco Sforza rose from the rank of private citizen to the rank of Duke of Milan; and it was because they feared the disgust and fatigue that his children fell from the rank of duke to the rank of private citizen.

One of the unfortunate consequences for a prince of neglecting his arms is that he comes to be despised; an abjection from which he must guard against in every respect, as I shall say below. He is, in fact, like an unarmed man, between whom and an armed man the disproportion is immense. Nor is it natural for the latter to willingly obey the former; and an unarmed master can never be safe among servants who are armed: the former is prey to spite, the latter to suspicion; and men who are driven by such feelings cannot live well together. Can a prince who understands nothing about the art of war win the esteem of his soldiers and have confidence in them? He must therefore apply himself constantly to this art, and deal with it mainly during peacetime, which he can do in two ways, i.e. by exercising his body and his mind equally. He will exercise his body, firstly by manoeuvring his troops properly, and secondly by hunting, which will harden him to fatigue and at the same time teach him to know the lay of the land, the elevation of the mountains, the direction of the valleys, the lay of the plains, the nature of the rivers and marshes, all things to which he must pay the greatest attention.

He will find two advantages in this: the first is that, knowing his country well, he will be able to defend it much better; the second is that knowledge of one country makes it much easier to know another, which it may be necessary to study; for example, the mountains, valleys, plains and rivers of Tuscany bear a great resemblance to those of other regions. This knowledge is also very important, and a prince who does not have it lacks one of the first qualities a captain should have, for it is through this knowledge that he can discover the enemy, take his lodgings, direct the march of his troops, make arrangements for battle and lay siege to advantage.

Among the praises heaped on Philopœmen, leader of the Achaeans, the historians praise him above all for the fact that he never thought of anything else but the art of war; so that, when he roamed the countryside with his friends, he often stopped to resolve questions he put to them, such as the following: "If the enemy were on this hill, and we were here, who would be posted more advantageously? How could we go to him safely and without creating disorder in our ranks? If we had to retreat, how would we go about it? If he withdrew himself, how could we pursue him? And so, as he went along, he learned with them about the various accidents of war that might occur; he collected their opinions; he set out his own, and supported it with various arguments. The result of this constant attention was that, in the conduct of armies, no accident could occur which he did not know how to remedy immediately.

As for exercising the mind, the prince should read the historians, consider the actions of illustrious men, examine their conduct in war, seek the causes of their victories and defeats, and thus study what he should imitate and what he should shun. Above all, he must do what many great men have done, who, taking some famous ancient hero as their model, constantly had before their eyes his actions and all his conduct, and took them as their rules. Thus it is said that Alexander the Great imitated Achilles, that Caesar imitated Alexander, and that Scipio took Cyrus as his model. Indeed, anyone who has read Xenophon's life of Cyrus will find in that of Scipio how much his proposed imitation contributed to his glory, and how much, as regards chastity, affability, humanity and liberality, he conformed to everything said about his model by Xenophon in his Cyropaedia.

This is what a wise prince must do, and how, during peacetime, far from remaining idle, he can guard against the accidents of fortune, so that, if it

55

turns against him, he is in a position to resist its blows.

CHAPTER XV. Of the things for which all men, and especially princes, are praised or blamed.

It remains to examine how a prince should use it and conduct himself, whether towards his subjects or towards his friends. So many writers have spoken of this that I may be accused of presumption if I speak of it again, especially as in dealing with this subject I shall be straying from the common path. But, in my intention to write something useful for those who will read me, it seemed to me that it would be better to focus on the reality of things than to indulge in vain speculation.

Many people have imagined republics and principalities the likes of which have never been seen or known. But what use are these imaginations? There is such a distance between the way we live and the way we should live, that by studying only the latter we learn rather to ruin ourselves than to preserve ourselves: and anyone who wants to show himself a good man in everything and everywhere cannot fail to perish in the midst of so many bad men.

A prince who wants to maintain himself must therefore learn not to be good all the time, and to use it well or badly, according to necessity.

Leaving aside, therefore, all that has been imagined about the duties of princes, and sticking to reality, I say that all men, when they are spoken of, and especially princes, who are more prominent, are attributed one of the following qualities, which are cited as a characteristic trait, and for which they are praised or blamed. Thus one is reputed to be generous and another miserable (I am using a Tuscan expression here, because in our language a miser is someone who is greedy and inclined to plunder, and we call someone miserable (misero) who refrains too much from using his property); one is beneficent and another greedy; one cruel and another compassionate; one without faith, and another faithful to his word; one effeminate and fearful, and another firm and courageous; one debonair, and another proud; one dissolute, and another chaste; one frank, and another cunning; one hard, and another easy; one grave, and another light; one religious, and another incredulous, etc..

It would undoubtedly be very good, and everyone will agree, if all the good qualities I have just mentioned were to be found in one prince. But as this is hardly possible, and as the human condition does not allow for it, he must at least have the prudence to avoid those shameful vices which would cause him to lose his States. As for the other vices, I advise him to avoid them if he can; but if he cannot, there will be no great disadvantage if he indulges in them with less restraint; he should not even fear being accused of certain faults without which it would be difficult for him to maintain himself; For, if we examine things carefully, we find that, just as there are certain qualities which seem to be virtues and which would ruin the prince, so there are others which seem to be vices, and which may nevertheless result in his preservation and well-being.

CHAPTER XVI. Of liberality and avarice.

Beginning with the first two qualities set out above, I say that it would be good for a prince to be reputed liberal; however, liberality may be exercised in such a way that it only harms him without any benefit; for if it is exercised with distinction, and according to the rules of wisdom, it will be little known, it will make little noise, and it will not even guarantee him against the imputation of the opposite quality.

If a prince wishes to gain a reputation in the world as a liberal, he must of necessity spare no kind of sumptuousness; this will oblige him to exhaust his treasury by this kind of expenditure; from which it will follow that, in order to preserve the reputation he has acquired, he will finally be forced to burden his people with extraordinary charges, to become a tax collector, and to do, in a word, everything that can be done to have money. So he will soon begin to be odious to his subjects, and as he becomes poorer, he will be held in much lower esteem. Thus, having, by his generosity, gratified very few individuals and displeased a very large number, the slightest embarrassment will be considerable for him, and the slightest setback will put him in danger: if, knowing his error, he wants to withdraw from it, he will immediately see the shame attached to the name of miser reflected back on him.

The prince, therefore, not being able, without unfortunate consequences, to practise liberality in such a way that it becomes well known, should, if he has any prudence, not be too apprehensive of the reputation of being miserly, especially as in time he will acquire the reputation of being liberal. Seeing, in fact, that his thrift makes his income sufficient and puts him in a position either to defend himself against his enemies or to carry out useful undertakings without overburdening his people, he will be considered liberal by all those, infinite in number, from whom he will take nothing; and the reproach of avarice will only be levelled at him by those few who do not share in his gifts.

In our time, we have only seen great things done by princes who were known to be avaricious; all the others have remained in obscurity. Pope

Julius II had earned himself a reputation for liberality in order to become pontiff, but afterwards he thought nothing of consolidating it, thinking only of being able to wage war against the king of France; a war which he waged, as did several others, without imposing any extraordinary taxes, because his constant thrift provided for all expenses. If the current king of Spain had been considered liberal, he would not have formed or carried out so many undertakings.

A prince who does not want to have to despoil his subjects in order to defend himself, and who does not want to make himself poor and despised for fear of becoming rapacious, must have little fear of being accused of avarice, since this is one of the bad qualities that make him reign.

If it is said that Caesar rose to the empire through his liberality, and that the reputation of a liberal has brought many people to the highest ranks, I reply: either you are already a prince, or you are in the process of becoming one. In the first case, liberality is harmful to you; in the second, you must necessarily have a reputation for it: and it was in this second case that Caesar found himself, aspiring to sovereign power in Rome. But if, having achieved this, he had lived much longer and had not moderated his spending, he himself would have overthrown his empire.

If it is insisted, and it is still said that several princes have reigned and achieved great things with their armies, and although they nevertheless had the reputation of being very liberal, I will reply: the prince spends either on his own good and that of his subjects, or on the good of others: in the first case he must be thrifty; in the second he cannot be too liberal.

For the prince who goes out to conquer with his armies, living off the spoils of war, plundering and taxing, and making use of the property of others, generosity is necessary, for without it he would not be followed by his soldiers. There is also nothing to prevent him from being a generous distributor, as Cyrus, Caesar and Alexander were, of what belongs neither to himself nor to his subjects. By lavishing the good of others, he need not fear diminishing his credit; on the contrary, he can only increase it: it is only the lavishness of his own good that could harm him.

Finally, generosity, more than anything else, devours itself; for as you exercise it, you lose the ability to exercise it again: you become poor, despised, or rapacious and hateful. Contempt and hatred are undoubtedly the most important pitfalls for princes to avoid. But liberality infallibly leads to both. It is wiser, therefore, to resign oneself to being called miserly, a quality which attracts only contempt without hatred, than to put oneself, in order to avoid this name, in the necessity of incurring the qualification of rapacious, which engenders contempt and hatred at the same time.

CHAPTER XVII. Of cruelty and mercy, and whether it is better to be loved than feared.

Continuing to follow the other qualities set out above, I say that every prince should wish to be known as merciful and not cruel. We must, however, be careful not to use clemency inappropriately. Caesar Borgia was reputed to be cruel, but his cruelty restored order and unity to the Romagna; it brought back tranquillity and obedience. It can also be said, if we consider things carefully, that he was more merciful than the Florentine people, who, to avoid being reproached for cruelty, allowed the city of Pistoia to be destroyed.

A prince should not therefore be afraid of this reproach when it comes to keeping his subjects united and loyal. By setting a few examples of rigour, you will be more merciful than those who, out of too much pity, allow disorders to arise from which murders and robberies ensue; for these disorders hurt society as a whole, instead of the rigours ordered by the prince falling only on individuals.

But it is above all to a new prince that it is impossible to reproach cruelty, because in new states the dangers are very much multiplied. This is the same reason that Virgil puts into Dido's mouth, when he has her say, to excuse the rigour of her government:

Res dura et regni novitas me talia cogunt

Moliri, et late fines custode tueri.

VIRGILE, Æneid, lib. 1.

He must, however, believe and act only with great maturity, not frighten himself, and follow in everything the advice of prudence, tempered by that of humanity; so that he is not short-sighted through over-confidence, and excessive distrust does not make him intolerable.

The question then arose: Is it better to be loved than feared, or feared than loved?

One might reply that the best thing would be to be both. But, as it is very difficult for the two things to exist together, I say that, if one should be lacking, it is more certain to be feared than to be loved. Indeed, it can generally be said of men that they are ungrateful, fickle, secretive, trembling in the face of danger and greedy for gain; that as long as you do them good, they are yours, that they offer you their blood, their possessions, their lives, their children, as long as, as I have said, peril is only available at a distance; but that when it approaches, they quickly turn away. The prince who relied entirely on their word, and who, in this confidence, did not take other measures, would soon be lost; for all these friendships, bought by largesse, and not granted by generosity and greatness of soul, are sometimes, it is true, well deserved, but they are not actually possessed; and, when the time comes to use them, they are always lacking. Let us add that we are much less afraid of offending someone who makes us love him than someone who makes us fear him; for love is held together by a bond of gratitude that is very weak for human perversity, and which yields to the slightest motive of personal interest; whereas fear results from the threat of punishment, and this fear never fades.

However, the prince who wishes to be feared must do so in such a way that, if he does not win affection, he does not attract hatred either; which, moreover, is not impossible; for it is quite possible to be feared and not hated at the same time; and this is also what he will surely achieve, by refraining from attacking either the property of his subjects or the honour of their wives. If it is necessary for him to kill someone, he must not decide to do so until there is a clear reason for it, and this act of rigour appears to be well justified. But above all, he must be all the more careful not to harm property, since men are more likely to forget the death of even a father than the loss of their patrimony, and moreover he will have more frequent opportunities to do so. A prince who has once given himself over to robbery always finds reasons and means to seize the property of his subjects that he only rarely has to spill their blood.

It is when the prince is at the head of his troops, and commands a multitude of soldiers, that he should be less than ever apprehensive of being reputed cruel; for, without this reputation, an army cannot be kept in order and prepared for any undertaking.

Among Annibal's admirable deeds, it has been particularly noted that, although his army was very large, and made up of a mixture of several very different kinds of men, waging war on the territory of others, there never arose, either in good or bad fortune, any dissension between the troops, or any movement of revolt against the general. Where did this come from? if not from that excessive cruelty which, combined with Annibal's other great qualities, made him both the veneration and the terror of his soldiers, and without which all his other qualities would have been insufficient. The writers who, while celebrating the actions of this illustrious man on the one hand, blamed on the other what had been the main cause of them, had not thought things through.

To convince ourselves that Annibal's other qualities would not have been enough for him, we need only consider what happened to Scipio, a man such as is almost impossible to find in modern times, or even in the history of all known times. The troops he commanded in Spain rose up against him, and this revolt could only be attributed to his excessive leniency, which had allowed the soldiers to take far more liberties than military discipline required. Fabius Maximus also criticised him for this in the Senate, where he described him as a corrupter of the Roman militia.

Moreover, the Locrians, tormented and ruined by one of his lieutenants, were unable to obtain any revenge from him, and the insolence of the lieutenant was not suppressed; another effect of his easy nature. Whereupon someone, wishing to accuse him in the senate, said: "That there were men who knew better not to commit faults than to correct those of others". But fortunately he himself was subject to the orders of the senate, so that this quality, which was harmful by nature, remained somewhat hidden, and was even still a subject of praise for him.

Returning, then, to the question at issue, I conclude that since men love as they please and fear as the prince pleases, the latter must rely rather on what depends on him than on what depends on others: it is only necessary that, as I have said, he take care not to attract hatred.

CHAPTER XVIII. How princes must keep their word.

Everyone understands how commendable it is for a prince to be true to his word and to always act frankly and without artifice. In our time, however, we have seen great things done by princes who paid little heed to this loyalty and who knew how to impose their will on men by trickery. We have seen these princes finally prevail over those who took loyalty as the basis of all their conduct.

There are two ways of fighting: either with laws, or with force. The first is suited to man, the second to beasts; but as the first is often not sufficient, we are obliged to resort to the other: a prince must therefore know how to act appropriately, both as a beast and as a man. This is what ancient writers taught allegorically when they recount how Achilles and several other heroes of antiquity were entrusted to the centaur Chiron, so that he could feed and raise them.

By this, in fact, and by this half-man, half-beast teacher, they meant that a prince must in some way have both natures, and that one needs to be supported by the other. If he is only a lion, he will not see the traps; if he is only a fox, he will not defend himself against the wolves; and he also needs to be a fox to see the traps, and a lion to scare off the wolves. Those who simply stick to being lions are very unskilled.

A well-advised prince must not fulfil his promise when doing so would be harmful to him, and when the reasons which led him to promise no longer exist: this is the precept to be given. But as they are wicked and will certainly not keep their word to you, why should you keep yours? And besides, can a prince lack legitimate reasons to colour the non-fulfilment of what he has promised?

On this subject, we can cite an infinite number of modern examples, and cite a very large number of peace treaties and agreements of all kinds, which have become useless because of the infidelity of the princes who concluded them. It can be seen that those who knew best how to act like foxes were those who prospered the most.

But for that, what is absolutely necessary is to know how to disguise this fox-like nature, and to master perfectly the art of simulating and dissimulating. Men are so blinded, so driven by the need of the moment, that a deceiver always finds someone who will let himself be deceived.

Among recent examples, there is one that I don't want to pass over in silence.

Alexander VI never did anything but deceive; he thought of nothing else, and he always had the opportunity and the means to do so. There was never a man who asserted a thing with more assurance, who backed his word with more oaths, and who kept them with less scruple: his deceptions always succeeded, however, because he knew the art perfectly.

So, to return to the good qualities set out above, it is not necessary for a prince to possess them all; but it is necessary for him to appear to have them. I would even dare to say that if he actually had them, and if he always showed them in his conduct, they could harm him, instead of it always being useful for him to have the appearance of them. It is always good, for example, to appear merciful, faithful, humane, religious and sincere; it is even good to be all of these in reality: but at the same time he must be sufficiently in control of himself to be able and to know how to show the opposite qualities when necessary.

It must be clearly understood that it is not possible for a prince, and especially a new prince, to observe in his conduct everything that makes men reputed to be good people, and that he is often obliged, in order to maintain the State, to act against humanity, against charity, even against religion. He must therefore have a mind flexible enough to turn to all things, as the wind and the accidents of fortune dictate; he must, as I have said, as long as he can, not stray from the path of good, but if necessary he must know how to enter the path of evil.

He must also take great care not to let slip a single word that does not exude the five qualities I have just named, so that when he is seen and heard he is believed to be full of gentleness, sincerity, humanity, honour and above all religion, which is also what it is most important to appear to be: for men in general judge more by their eyes than by their hands, all being able to see and few to touch. Everyone sees what you look like; few know in depth what you are, and this small number will not dare to speak out against the opinion of the majority, which is still supported by the majesty of sovereign power.

Moreover, in the actions of men, and especially of princes, which cannot be scrutinised in a court of law, what is considered is the result. Let the prince think only of preserving his life and his state: if he succeeds, all the means he has taken will be judged honourable and praised by everyone. The vulgar is always seduced by appearances and events: and do not the vulgar make the world? The few are only listened to when the many do not know what side to take or what to base their judgement on.

In our time, we have seen a prince[7] whom it is not appropriate to name, who never preached anything but peace and good faith, but who, if he had always respected both, would probably not have kept his States and his reputation.

CHAPTER XIX. That we must avoid being despised and hated.

After having dealt specifically with those qualities that I consider to be the most important, I will speak more briefly about the others, limiting myself to the general point that the prince must carefully avoid anything that would make him odious and contemptible, in return for which he will have done all that he had to do, and he will no longer find any danger in the other reproaches that he might incur.

What would make him especially odious would be, as I said, to be rapacious and to attack either the property of his subjects or the honour of their wives. Provided that these two things, property and honour, are respected, ordinary people are content, and the only thing left to fight against is the ambition of a small number of individuals, which is easy to suppress and for which there are a thousand means.

What can make people despise him is to appear inconstant, light, effeminate, pusillanimous, irresolute, all things from which the prince must keep away as from a pitfall, ensuring that in all his actions there is greatness, courage, gravity, firmness; that they be convinced, as regards the particular affairs of his subjects, that his decisions are irrevocable, and that this conviction be established in their minds in such a way that no one dares to think of deceiving or circumventing him.

The prince who gave this idea of himself is highly regarded, and it is difficult for anyone to conspire against someone who is so highly regarded; it is even difficult for anyone to attack him when they know that he has great qualities and is respected by his own people.

A prince must be concerned with two things: the interior of his States and the conduct of his subjects are the object of one; the exterior and the designs of the surrounding powers are the object of the other. For the latter, the way to protect oneself is to have good weapons and good friends; and one will always have good friends when one has good weapons: Moreover, as long as the prince is safe and calm on the outside, he will also be so on the inside, unless he has already been disturbed by some conspiracy; and if even on the outside some enterprise is formed against him, he will find on the inside, as I have already said that Nabis, tyrant of Sparta, found them, the means to resist any attack, provided, however, that he has behaved and governed in accordance with what I have observed, and moreover that he does not lose heart.

As for the subjects, what the prince may fear from them, when he is at peace on the outside, is that they may secretly conspire against him; but in this respect he is already well protected when he has avoided being hated and despised, and has ensured that the people are pleased with him; something which it is absolutely necessary to overcome, as I have established. This is, in fact, the surest guarantee against conspiracies; for he who conspires always believes that the death of the prince will be pleasing to the people: if he thought that it would afflict them, he would be careful not to conceive such a plan, which presents very great and very numerous difficulties.

We know from experience that many conjurations have been formed, but that very few have had a successful outcome. A man cannot conjure alone: he must have associates, and he can only look for them among those he believes to be discontented. Now, by entrusting a project of this nature to a malcontent, we provide him with the means to put an end to his discontent; for he can count on being amply rewarded by revealing the secret: and as he sees in it an assured profit, whereas conspiracy presents him with nothing but uncertainty and danger, he must have, in order not to betray, either a very lively friendship for the conspirator, or a very obstinate hatred for the prince. In short, the conspirator is always troubled by suspicion, jealousy and fear of punishment; whereas the prince has for him the majesty of the empire, the authority of the laws, the support of his friends, and everything that makes up the defence of the State; And if all this is combined with the goodwill of the people, it is impossible for anyone to be so foolhardy as to conspire; for, in this case, the conspirator not only has to fear the dangers that precede the execution, he must also fear those that will follow, against which, with the people as his enemy, he will have no refuge.

An infinite number of examples could be cited, but I will limit myself to just one that our fathers witnessed.

Messire Annibal Bentivogli, grandfather of the present Messer Annibal, being Prince of Bologna, was murdered by the Canneschi, following a conspiracy they had hatched against him: all that remained of his family was Messer Giovanni, a young child still in the cradle. But the affection that the people of Bologna had for the House of Bentivogli was such that immediately after the murder they rose up and massacred all the Canneschi. This affection went even further: as after the death of Messer Annibal, there was no one left who could govern the State, and the Bolognese having heard that there was a man born of the Bentivogli family living in Florence, where he passed for the son of a craftsman, they went looking for him and entrusted him with the government, which he kept until Messer Giovanni was old enough to hold the reins of State himself.

Once again, then, a prince who is loved by his people has little to fear from conspiracies; but if he is hated by them, everything, both things and men, is for him to fear. This is why well-regulated governments and wise princes always take great care to satisfy the people and keep them happy without upsetting the great ones too much: this is one of the most important things they can do.

Among the well-organised kingdoms of our time is France, where there are a large number of good institutions capable of maintaining the independence and security of the king; institutions among which that of parliament and its authority ranks first. Indeed, the man who organised France in this way, seeing, on the one hand, the ambition and insolent pride of the great, and how necessary it was to repress them; considering, on the other hand, the general hatred of them, hatred engendered by the fear they inspired, and consequently wanting to ensure their safety as well, thought it appropriate not to leave this to the king alone, so that he would not have to incur the hatred of the nobles by favouring the people, and that of the people by favouring the nobles. This is why he thought it good to establish the third authority of a court which could, without any unfortunate consequences for the king, lower the great and protect the small. Such an institution was undoubtedly the best, wisest and most appropriate thing that could be done for the safety of the prince and the kingdom.

From this we can also draw another remark: that the prince must unburden himself to others of those parts of the administration which may be odious, and reserve exclusively for himself those of graces; in a word, I repeat, he must have respect for the great, but avoid being hated by the people.

If you look at the lives and deaths of several Roman emperors, you will perhaps think you see examples contrary to what I have just said, for you will find some who, having always behaved wisely and shown great qualities, never failed to lose the empire, or even to perish as victims of conspiracies formed against them.

To answer this objection, I shall examine the character and conduct of some of these emperors, and show that the causes of their downfall do not present anything that does not accord with what I have established. I will also give some thoughts on what the events of those times can offer that is remarkable to those who read history. However, I shall confine myself to the emperors who succeeded each other from Marcus Aurelius to Maximin: They are: Marcus Aurelius, Commodus his son, Pertinax, Didius Julianus, Septimius-Severus, Antonin-Caracalla, his son, Macrin, Heliogabalus, Alexander-Severus and Maximin.

The first observation to make is that, whereas in other states the prince has only to contend with the ambition of the great and the insolence of the people, the Roman emperors had to overcome a third difficulty, that of defending themselves against the cruelty and avarice of the soldiers; a difficulty such as was the cause of the ruin of several of these princes. It is very difficult, in fact, to please both the soldiers and the people; for the people like rest, and consequently, a moderate prince: the soldiers, on the other hand, demand that he be warlike, insolent, greedy and cruel; they even want him to show himself such towards the people, in order to have double pay, and to satisfy their avarice and cruelty. From this also came the ruin of all those emperors who did not have, either by their natural qualities or by their acquired qualities, the ascendancy necessary to contain both the people and the men of war. From this also came the fact that most of them, and especially those who were new princes, seeing the difficulty of satisfying such opposing moods, decided to please the soldiers without worrying about the oppression of the people.

This, moreover, was a necessary course to take; for princes, who cannot avoid being hated by someone, must first try not to be hated by the multitude; and, if they cannot succeed in this, they must make every effort not to be hated at least by the most powerful class. It was for this reason, too, that the emperors, who as new princes needed extraordinary support, attached themselves far more readily to the soldiers than to the people; yet this was only useful to them insofar as they were able to maintain their ascendancy over them.

It is as a consequence of all that I have just said that of the three emperors Marcus Aurelius, Pertinax and Alexander Severus, who lived with wisdom and moderation, who were friends of justice, enemies of cruelty, humane and beneficent, only the first did not come to an unfortunate end. But if he lived and died always honoured, it was because, having inherited the empire by right of succession, he owed it neither to the men of war nor to the people, and because, moreover, his great and numerous virtues made him so respected that he was always able to keep all the orders of the State within the bounds of duty, without being either hated or despised.

As for Pertinax, the soldiers, against whose will he had been appointed emperor, could not bear the discipline he wanted to re-establish after the licentiousness in which they had lived under Commodus: he was therefore hated. This hatred was compounded by contempt for his old age, and he died almost as soon as he began to reign. Hence it follows, as I have said, that a prince who wishes to maintain himself is often obliged to be no good; for when the class of subjects he believes he needs, whether people, soldiers or grandees, is corrupt, he must satisfy them at all costs if he is not to have them against him; and then good deeds do more harm than good.

Finally, with regard to Alexander Severus, his goodness was such that, among the praises he has received, it has been noted that, during the fourteen years of his reign, no one was put to death without a regular trial. However, as he had come to be regarded as an effeminate man who allowed himself to be ruled by his mother, and as a result had fallen into contempt, his army conspired against him and massacred him.

If we now turn to the emperors who showed quite opposite qualities, that is to say Commodus, Septimius-Severus, Antonin-Caracalla and Maximin, we shall see that they were very cruel and insatiably greedy; that, to satisfy the soldiers, they spared the people no kind of oppression and insult, and that they all came to an unhappy end, with the sole exception of Severus, who, through the greatness of his courage and other eminent qualities, was able, by retaining the affection of the soldiers, and although he burdened the people with taxes, to reign happily always; for this greatness made him admired by all, in such a way that the people remained stunned and astonished, and the soldiers were respectful and satisfied. Severus, moreover, behaved very skilfully as a new prince: that is why I shall pause for a moment to show how well he knew how to act like a fox and a lion, two animals which, as I have said, a prince must know how to assume.

Knowing the cowardice of Didius Julianus, who had just been proclaimed emperor, he persuaded the troops at whose head he was then in Pannonia that it was worthy of them to go to Rome to avenge the death of Pertinax, whose throat had been slit by the imperial guard; Without revealing the secret plans he had for the empire, he seized this pretext, hastened to Rome with his army and appeared in Italy before anyone knew he was leaving. On arriving in Rome, he was proclaimed emperor by the terrified Senate, and Julianus was massacred. Once this first step had been taken, he still had two obstacles to overcome in order to take control of the whole state: one in the East, where Niger had been proclaimed emperor by the Asian armies he commanded; the other in the West, where Albin also aspired to the empire. As he saw too much danger in declaring himself against these two competitors at the same time, he planned to attack Niger and deceive Albin. Consequently, he wrote to Albin that, having been appointed emperor by the senate, it was his intention to share the imperial dignity with him: he therefore sent him the title of Caesar and had him appointed as his colleague by a senate decree. Albinus allowed himself to be seduced by these demonstrations, which he believed to be sincere. But when Severus had killed Niger, having defeated him, and the troubles in the East had subsided, he returned to Rome and complained in the senate about Albin's conduct, accusing him of having shown little gratitude for all the benefits he had bestowed on him, and of having secretly attempted to assassinate him; and he concluded by saying that he could not avoid marching against him to punish him for his ingratitude. He suddenly went to attack him in Gaul, where he took his empire and his life.

Such was the conduct of this prince. If we follow all his actions step by step, we will see everywhere the boldness of a lion and the shrewdness of a fox; we will see him feared and revered by his subjects, and cherished even by his soldiers: we will therefore not be surprised that, although he was a new man, he was able to maintain himself in such a vast empire; for his high reputation always defended him against the hatred that his continual exactions might have kindled in the hearts of his peoples.

Antonin-Caracalla, his son, also had eminent qualities that made him admired by the people and cherished by the soldiers. His skill in the art of war, his disdain for expensive food and the delights of indulgence won him the affection of the troops; but his cruelty, his unheard-of ferocity, the many murders he inflicted on some of the citizens of Rome on a daily basis, the general massacre of the inhabitants of Alexandria, made him the object of universal abhorrence: those around him soon had to fear for themselves, and a centurion killed him in the midst of his army.

An important observation follows from this fact: it is that a prince cannot avoid death when a man firm and hardened in his vengeance has resolved to destroy him; for whoever despises his own life is master of that of others. But as these dangers are rare, they are consequently less to be feared. All that the prince can and must do in this respect is to be careful not to offend seriously any of those whom he employs and has around him in his service; this care was not taken by Caracalla, who had unjustly killed a brother of the centurion by whom he was killed, who threatened him daily himself, and who nevertheless kept him in his guard. This was undoubtedly a temerity that could only lead to his ruin, as events proved.

As for Commodus, the son and heir of Marcus Aurelius, it was certainly easy for him to maintain his position in the empire: all he had to do was follow in his father's footsteps to please the people and the soldiers. But, giving in to his cruel and ferocious nature, he wanted to crush the people with his plunder with impunity; he decided to pamper the troops and let them live in licentiousness. Moreover, forgetting all care for his dignity, he was often seen going down into the arena to fight with the gladiators, and indulging in the turpitudes most unworthy of imperial majesty. He made himself vile in the eyes of his soldiers. Thus, having become the object of both hatred and contempt, they conspired against him and he was slaughtered.

It only remains for me to talk about Maximin. He possessed all the qualities that make a man of war. After the death of Alexander Severus, of whom I spoke earlier, the armies, disgusted with the weakness of the latter prince, raised Maximin to the empire; but he did not hold it for long. Two things contributed to making him despised and hated. The first was the lowliness of his first state: as a herdsman in Thrace, this extraction, known to everyone, made him vile in everyone's eyes. The second was the reputation for cruelty which he immediately acquired; for, without going to Rome to take possession of the imperial throne, he had his lieutenants commit numerous acts of rigour there, as well as in all parts of the empire. On the one hand, the state, indignant at the lowliness of his origins, and on the other, aroused by the fear inspired by his barbarities, rose up against him. The signal was given by Africa. Immediately the Senate and the people followed this example, which was not long in being imitated by the rest of Italy. Soon this general conspiracy was joined by that of his troops: they laid siege to Aquileia; but, put off by the difficulties of the siege, tired of his cruelties, and beginning to fear him less since they saw him facing a multitude of enemies, they decided to massacre him.

I will not stop now to talk about Heliogabalus, Macrinus or Didius Julianus, men so vile that they only appeared on the throne. But, coming immediately to the conclusion of my speech, I say that modern princes find one less difficulty in their administration: that of extraordinarily satisfying the people of war. Indeed, they must undoubtedly have some regard for them, but there is no great embarrassment in that, because none of these princes has the large corps of troops that are still in existence and that have been amalgamated, as it were, by the passage of time with the government and administration of the provinces, as were the Roman armies. The emperors were obliged to please the soldiers rather than the people, because the soldiers were the most powerful; but today it is the people that the princes have above all to satisfy. The only exceptions in this respect are the Great Lord of the Turks and the Sudan.

I exclude the Great Lord, because he always has around him a corps of twelve thousand infantry and fifteen thousand cavalry; these corps make up his security and strength, and consequently he must in all things, and without thinking of the people, spare and keep their affection.

I exclude the Sudan, because as its states are entirely in the hands of the people of war, it must conciliate their friendship, without embarrassing itself with the people.

It should be noted, in this connection, that the state of Sudan differs from all others, and bears little resemblance to anything other than the Christian pontificate, which can be called neither a hereditary principality nor a new principality. Indeed, on the death of the prince, it is not his children who inherit and reign after him; but his successor is elected by those to whom this election belongs; and moreover, as this order of things is consecrated by its antiquity, it does not present the difficulties of new principalities: the prince, indeed, is new, but the institutions are ancient, which makes him received just as if he were a hereditary prince. Let us return to our subject.

Anyone who reflects on all that I have just said will see that the ruin of the emperors I have spoken of was indeed caused by hatred or contempt, and he will at the same time understand why, some acting in a certain way and others in a quite different way, only one on either side ended happily, while all the others ended their days miserably. He will understand that it was useless and even fatal for Pertinax and Alexander Severus, new princes, to want to imitate Marcus Aurelius, hereditary prince; and that, similarly, Caracalla, Commodus and Maximin harmed themselves by wanting to imitate Severus, because they did not have the great qualities necessary to be able to follow in his footsteps.

I also say that a new prince can and must not imitate either Marcus Aurelius or Severus, but must take from the example of Severus what he needs to establish his power, and from that of Marcus Aurelius what he can use to maintain the stability and glory of a long-established and consolidated empire.

Chapter XX. Whether fortresses, and several other things that princes often do, are useful or harmful to them

Princes have employed various means to maintain their states securely. Some have disarmed their subjects; some others have maintained the division of parties in the countries under their control: some have liked to foment enmities against themselves; some have also endeavoured to win over those who, at the beginning of their reign, had seemed suspicious; finally, some have built fortresses, while others have demolished them. It is impossible to form a definite opinion on these various means without examining the particular circumstances of the State to which it is intended to apply one of them. Nevertheless, I am going to talk about them generally and as the subject requires.

It has never happened that a new prince has disarmed his subjects; on the contrary, he who found them without arms gave them some, because he thought that these arms would be his; that by giving them, he would make those who were suspicious loyal; that the others would maintain their loyalty, and that all, finally, would become his supporters. It is true that not all his subjects can bear arms; but the prince must not fear, by rewarding those who take up arms, to upset the others in such a way that he will have cause for concern: the former will be grateful for the reward, and the latter will see fit to treat better those who have served more and exposed themselves to more danger.

A prince who disarmed his subjects would begin to offend them, by showing them that he mistrusted their loyalty; and this mistrust, whatever the object, would inspire hatred against him. Moreover, unable to remain unarmed, he would be forced to have recourse to a mercenary militia; and I have already said what this militia is, which, even if it were good, could never be large enough to defend him against powerful enemies and irritated subjects. So, as I have already said, any prince new to a new principality has never failed to organise an armed force. History provides numerous examples of this.

It is when a prince has acquired a new state, which he adds to the one he already possesses, that it is important for him to disarm the subjects of the new state, with the exception, however, of those who declared themselves for him at the time of the acquisition: even so, he should make it easy for them to give in to softness and effeminacy, and he should organise things in such a way that there is no army left but his own soldiers, living in his old state and close to his person.

Our ancestors, and particularly those who were considered wise, commonly said that Pistoia should be contained by means of parties, and Pisa by means of fortresses. They also took care to maintain division in some of the countries under their control, in order to keep them more easily. This may have been good at a time when there was a sort of balance in Italy, but it seems to me that it would no longer be advisable today, because I don't think that divisions could be good for anything. It even seems to me that, when the enemy approaches, divided countries are infallibly and soon lost; for the weak party will join the outside forces, and the other will no longer be able to resist. The Venetians, who I believe thought like our ancestors in this respect, maintained the Guelph and Ghibelline parties in the cities under their domination. To be sure, they did not allow things to escalate to the point of bloodshed, but they fomented enough division and quarrels to keep the inhabitants so busy that they did not think of leaving their obedience. Nevertheless, they found it difficult, and when they lost the battle of Vailà, these same towns immediately became bold and shook off the yoke of Venetian authority.

A prince who employs such means shows his weakness, and a strong government will never tolerate divisions: while they may be of some use during peacetime, by making it easier to keep his subjects in check, as soon as war breaks out, they can only be harmful.

Princes undoubtedly become greater when they overcome all the obstacles to their elevation. So when fortune wishes to make a new prince, who needs to acquire a reputation more than a hereditary prince, greater, it creates around him a crowd of enemies against whom it pushes him, in order to provide him with the opportunity to triumph, and thus gives him the opportunity to rise by means of a ladder that his enemies themselves provide him with. This is why many people have thought that a wise prince should, if he can, skilfully foster some enmity, so that by overcoming it he increases his own greatness.

Princes, and particularly new princes, have found that men who, when they first established their power, had seemed suspicious, were more loyal and useful to them than those who had initially shown themselves to be devoted. Pandolfo Petrucci, prince of Siena, preferred to employ in his government those whom he had initially suspected.

It would be difficult, on this subject, to give general rules, and everything depends on particular circumstances. I will therefore limit myself to saying that, for men who, at the beginning of a new principality, were enemies, and who find themselves in such a position that they need support to maintain themselves, the prince will always be able to win them over very easily, and that, for their part, they will be forced to serve him with all the more zeal and fidelity, as they will feel that they have to erase, through their services, the bad idea that they had given him reason to take of them. They will therefore be more useful to him than those who, having neither the same motives nor the same fear, may carelessly look after his interests.

And, since my subject brings me to this point, I would also point out to any new prince who has seized the principality by means of internal intelligences, that he must carefully consider the motives of those who have acted in his favour; for, if they have not done so out of natural affection, but only because they were dissatisfied with his present government, the new prince will have extreme difficulty in retaining their friendship, since it will be impossible for him to please them.

If we reflect on the examples that ancient and modern times offer us in this respect, we will see that it is much easier for the new prince to win over those who were his enemies at first, because they were satisfied with the old state of affairs, than those who became his friends and favoured him, because they were dissatisfied.

It has generally been the practice of princes, in order to maintain themselves, to build fortresses, either in order to prevent revolts, or in order to have a safe place of refuge against a first attack. I approve of this system, because it was followed by the ancients. Nowadays, however, we have seen Niccolo Vitelli demolish two fortresses in Città di Castello in order to maintain his possession of the country. Similarly, Guido Ubaldo, Duke of Urbino, on returning to his duchy, from which he had been expelled by Caesar Borgia, destroyed all the citadels there to the foundations, thinking that this measure would make it less likely that he would be dispossessed a second time. Finally, the Bentivogli, who had been re-established in Bologna, did the same. Fortresses are therefore useful or not, depending on the circumstances, and even if they are useful at one time, they are harmful at another. Here is what can be said about them.

A prince who fears his subjects more than foreigners should build fortresses; but he should not have any if he fears foreigners more than his subjects: the castle of Milan, built by Francesco Sforza, has done more harm to the house of this prince than any disorder that has arisen in his states. The best fortress a prince can have is the affection of his people: if he is hated, all the fortresses he can have will not save him; for if his people once take up arms, they will always find foreigners to support them.

In our time, we have only seen the Countess of Forli take advantage of a fortress where, after the murder of her husband, the Count of Girolamo, she could find refuge from the uprising of the people, and wait for help to be sent to her from Milan so that she could regain her States. But, at that time, circumstances were such that no foreigner could support the people. Moreover, this same fortress was of little use to her later, when she was attacked by Caesar Borgia, and the people, who hated her, were able to join forces with this enemy. On this last occasion, as on the first, it would have been much better for her not to be hated than to have fortresses.

From all this, I approve equally of those who build fortresses and those who do not; but I will always blame anyone who, relying on this defence, does not fear to incur the hatred of the people.

Chapter XXI. How a prince must behave to acquire a reputation.

To undertake great undertakings, to set rare examples by his actions, is what most illustrates a prince. In our time, we can cite Ferdinand of Aragon, currently King of Spain, as one such illustrious prince. He can be called a new prince, as it were, because, although at first he was a king of little power, fame and glory made him the first king of Christendom.

If we examine his actions, we will find them all stamped with the character of greatness, and some will even seem to stray from the ordinary route. From the beginning of his reign, he attacked the kingdom of Granada, and this undertaking became the foundation of his greatness. It also provided him with the means to occupy the ambitions of the great men of Castile, who, entirely absorbed in this war, did not think of innovating, while he, for his part, acquired over them, through his fame, an ascendancy of which they were unaware. What's more, the money he received from the Church and the money he raised from the people enabled him to maintain the armies which, formed by this long series of wars, made him so respected afterwards. After this undertaking, and still cloaking himself in the mantle of religion in order to achieve greater things, he applied himself with pious cruelty to persecuting the Moors and purging his kingdom of them: an admirable example that cannot be meditated on too much. Finally, under the same pretext of religion, he attacked Africa; then he brought his arms to Italy; and, lastly, he waged war against France: so that he never ceased to form and execute great plans, always keeping the spirits of his subjects in admiration and in anticipation of events. All these actions, moreover, followed on from one another and were linked to one another in such a way that there was neither time to breathe nor the means to interrupt their course.

What can also serve to illustrate a prince is to offer, as did Messer Barnabo Visconti, Duke of Milan, in his internal administration, and when the occasion arises, singular examples that give much to talk about in terms of how to punish or reward those who, in civil life, have committed great crimes or rendered great services; it is to act, in every circumstance, in such a way that one is forced to regard him as superior to ordinary men.

We also esteem a prince who is openly friendly or hostile, that is to say who knows how to declare himself openly and unreservedly for or against someone, which is always a more useful choice than remaining neutral.

Indeed, when two neighbouring powers come to blows, one of two things happens: either they are or they are not such that you have something to fear from the one that will remain victorious. In either case, it will be useful for you to have declared yourself openly and to have waged war frankly. Here are the reasons why.

In the first case, if you do not declare yourself, you will remain the prey of the victorious power, to the satisfaction and contentment of the vanquished power, which will have no reason to defend you or even to give you asylum. As for the second, why should it welcome you, who refused to take up arms on its behalf and run after its fortunes?

Antiochus had come to Greece, where he was called by the Aetolians, with a view to driving out the Romans, and sent orators to the Achaeans, allies of the latter people, inviting them to remain neutral. The Romans also sent speakers to urge them to take up arms on their behalf. The matter being discussed in the council of the Achaeans, and Antiochus' envoys insisting on neutrality, those of the Romans replied, addressing the Achaeans: "As for the advice we give you to take no part in our war, and which we present to you as the best and most useful for your country, there is none that could be more harmful to you; for if you follow it, you remain the prize of the victor without having gained the slightest glory for yourself, and without any obligation to you. "

A government must count on the fact that always the belligerent party which is not its friend will ask it to remain neutral, and that the friendly party will want it to declare itself by taking up arms.

This party of neutrality is the one most often embraced by irresolute princes, frightened by present dangers, and it is the one that most often leads to their ruin.

If you have shown yourself to be resolutely and vigorously in favour of one of the two parties, they will have nothing to fear for you if they remain victorious, even if they are powerful enough for you to be at their discretion; for they will be obliged to you: they will have contracted some bond of friendship with you; and men are never so devoid of any sense of honour that they want to overwhelm those with whom they have such relations, and thus set an example of the blackest ingratitude. Moreover, victories are never so complete that the victor can believe himself free from all consideration, and above all from all justice. But if this belligerent party, for which you have declared yourself, is defeated, you can at least count on being helped as much as possible, and on being associated with a fortune that can be re-established.

In the second hypothesis, i.e. when the two rival powers are not such that you have anything to fear from the one that will remain victorious, prudence advises you even more to declare yourself for one of the two. What will happen? It is that you will have ruined one of these powers by the means and with the help of another which, if it had been wise, should have supported it, and which will find itself at your discretion after the victory which your support must infallibly lead it to obtain.

On this point, moreover, I observe that a prince must never, as I have already said, join forces with another more powerful than himself to attack a third, unless he is forced to do so by necessity, because victory would put him at the discretion of this other more powerful one; and princes must, in all things, avoid finding themselves at the discretion of others. The Venetians joined forces with France against the Duke of Milan, and this association, which they could have avoided, led to their ruin.

If such an association is inevitable, as it was for the Florentines when the Pope and Spain marched their troops against Lombardy, then it must be decided, whatever happens.

Moreover, a government must not assume that it will always take only very certain courses of action: on the contrary, it must be thought that there is no course of action in which there is not some uncertainty. Such is indeed the order of things that we never seek to avoid one disadvantage without falling into another; and prudence consists only in examining and judging the disadvantages and taking as good what is the least bad.

A prince must also show himself to be a lover of talent, and honour those who distinguish themselves in their profession. He must encourage his subjects and enable them to exercise their industry in peace, whether in trade, agriculture or any other kind of work in which men engage; so that there is no one who refrains either from improving his possessions for fear that they will be taken away from him, or from undertaking any trade for fear of having to suffer atrocities. He must give hope of rewards to those who undertake such ventures, as well as to all those who think of increasing the wealth and grandeur of the State. He must also, at certain appropriate times of the year, entertain the people with festivals and shows; and, as all the citizens of a State are divided into communities of arts or tribes, he cannot show too much consideration for these guilds; he will sometimes appear at their assemblies, and will always show humanity and magnificence, without compromising the majesty of his rank, a majesty that must not abandon him under any circumstances.

Chapter XXII. The secretaries of princes.

It is not a matter of little importance for a prince to choose his ministers, who are good or bad depending on whether he is more or less wise himself. So, when we want to assess his ability, we first judge by the people around him. If they are skilful and loyal, we always assume that he is wise himself, since he has been able to discern their skill and ensure their loyalty; but we think quite differently if these people are not so; and the choice he made of them must have been his first operation, so the mistake he made is a very unfortunate omen. All those who learned that Pandolfo Petrucci, Prince of Siena, had chosen Messer Antonio da Venafro as his minister, judged that Pandolfo was a very wise and enlightened prince.

Three orders of mind may be distinguished, namely: those who understand by themselves, those who understand when others demonstrate to them, and finally those who understand neither by themselves nor by the help of others. The first are superior minds, the second good minds, and the third no minds at all. If Pandolfo was not of the first order, he must certainly at least have been of the second, and that was enough; for a prince who is in a position, if not to imagine, at least to judge what another does and says right or wrong, knows how to discern the good or bad actions of his minister, to favour some, to repress others, to leave no hope of being able to deceive him, and thus to keep the minister himself in line with his duty.

Moreover, if a prince wants a definite rule for knowing his ministers, we can give him this: If you see a minister thinking more of himself than of you, and seeking his own interest in all his actions, judge at once that he is not what he should be, and that he cannot deserve your confidence; for the man who has the administration of a State in his hands must never think of himself but must always think of the prince, and speak to him only about what is in the interest of the State.

But the prince must also think of his minister, if he wants to keep him faithful at all times; he must surround him with consideration, shower him with riches, include him in all honours and dignities, so that he has no reason to wish for more; at the height of favour, he must fear the slightest change, and be convinced that he could not support himself without the support of the prince.

When the prince and the minister are as I say, they can surrender to each other with confidence: if they are not, the end will be equally unfortunate for both.

Chapter XXIII. How to avoid flatterers.

I will not neglect to mention an important article, and an error from which it is very difficult for princes to defend themselves, if they are not endowed with great prudence, and if they do not have the art of making good choices; I am referring to the flatterers with whom courts are always full.

If, on the one hand, princes blinded by self-love find it difficult not to allow themselves to be corrupted by this plague, on the other hand, they run one danger in fleeing from it: that of falling into contempt. Indeed, there is only one good way to guard against flattery, and that is to make it clear that you cannot displease them by telling them the truth: if anyone can freely tell a prince what he believes to be true, he will soon cease to be respected.

What course, then, can he take to avoid any inconvenience? If he is prudent, he should choose a few wise men from his States and give them, but them alone, complete freedom to tell him the truth, limiting himself to the matters about which he will question them. He must, moreover, consult them on everything, listen to their opinions and then resolve the matter himself; he must also conduct himself, either towards all the advisers together or towards each of them individually, in such a way as to persuade them that they are all the more agreeable to him the more frankly they speak; finally, he must not wish to hear any other person, act according to the decision he has made and stick to it firmly.

The prince who uses it otherwise is ruined by flatterers, or he is prone to constant variation, dragged down by the diversity of advice; which greatly diminishes his esteem. I will cite a recent example. The priest Lucas, agent of Maximilian, now Emperor, said of this prince "that he never took advice from anyone, and that he never did anything according to his own will". Maximilian, in fact, is a very secretive man, who confides in no one and asks for no advice; but as his plans become known as they are put into effect, they are immediately contradicted by those around him, and out of weakness he allows himself to be led astray: hence what he does one day he undoes the next; we never know what he desires or what he intends, and we cannot count on any of his decisions.

A prince must therefore always take advice, but he must do so when he wants to, and not when others want him to; he must not even allow anyone to be so bold as to give him his opinion on anything, unless he asks for it; but he must also not be too reserved in his questions, and he must listen patiently to the truth, and when someone is prevented, by certain considerations, from telling him, he must show his displeasure.

Those who claim that this or that prince who appears wise is not in fact wise, because the wisdom he shows does not come from himself, but from the good advice he receives, are making a great mistake; For it is a general rule, and one that never deceives, that a prince who is not wise in himself cannot be well advised, unless chance has placed him entirely in the hands of some very skilful man, who alone masters and governs him; in which case, moreover, he may, to be sure, be well led, but only for a short time, for the driver will soon seize power. But outside this situation, and when he is obliged to have several advisers, the prince who lacks wisdom will always find them divided among themselves and will not know how to unite them. Each of these advisers will think only of his own interests, and he will be in no position either to take them up again or even to judge them: from which it follows that he will never have anything but bad advisers, because they will not be forced by necessity to become good. In a word, good advice, wherever it comes from, is the fruit of the prince's wisdom, and this wisdom is not the fruit of good advice.

Chapter XXIV. Why the Princes of Italy lost their States.

The new prince who conforms his conduct to all that we have noted will be regarded as old, and soon he will even be more surely and more firmly established than if his power had been consecrated by time. Indeed, the actions of a new prince are much more closely scrutinised than those of an old prince; and when they are judged to be virtuous, they win and endear him to many more hearts than the seniority of the race could do; for men are much more moved by the present than by the past; and when their present situation satisfies them, they enjoy it without thinking of anything else; they are even very willing to uphold and defend the prince, provided he does not fail himself.

The prince will therefore have a double glory, that of having founded a new State, and that of having adorned and consolidated it with good laws, good weapons, good allies and good examples; whereas on the contrary, there will be a double shame for the one who, born on the throne, let it be lost by his lack of wisdom.

If we consider the conduct of the various princes of Italy who, in our time, have lost their States, such as the King of Naples, the Duke of Milan and others, we will first find a common fault to reproach them with, namely that concerning military forces, which has been discussed at length above. Secondly, we will recognise that they had attracted the hatred of the people, or that in possessing their friendship, they had failed to secure the support of the great. Without such faults, states powerful enough to field an army would not be lost.

Philip of Macedonia, not the father of Alexander the Great, but the man who was defeated by T. Quintus Flaminius, possessed only a small state compared with the greatness of the Roman republic and of Greece, by which he was attacked; nevertheless, as he was a skilful captain, and had known how to win over the people and secure the support of the great, he found himself in a position to sustain the war for several years; and if, in the end, he had to lose some cities, at least he kept his kingdom.

Let those of our princes who, after a long possession, have been stripped of their States, not blame fortune, but blame their own cowardice. Having never thought, in times of tranquillity, that things could change, similar in this to the common men who, during the calm, do not worry about the storm, they thought, when adversity arose, not to defend themselves, but to flee, hoping to be recalled by their peoples, who would have grown tired of the insolence of the conqueror. Such a course of action may be a good one to take when there is no other; but it is shameful to be reduced to it: you do not let yourself fall in the hope of being lifted up by someone. Moreover, it is not certain that in this case a prince will be recalled in this way; and, if he is, it will not be with great safety for him, because such a kind of defence degrades him and does not depend on his person. Now there is no good, certain and lasting defence for a prince, except that which depends on himself and his own worth.

Chapter XXV. How much power fortune has in human affairs, and how it can be resisted.

I am not unaware that many people have thought and still think that God and fortune govern the things of this world in such a way that all human prudence cannot stop or regulate their course: from which one may conclude that it is useless to concern oneself with so much trouble, and that there is nothing to do but to submit and let everything be governed by fate. This opinion has spread in our time mainly as a consequence of the variety of great events we have mentioned, which we are still witnessing, and which it was impossible for us to foresee: so I am inclined to share it.

Nevertheless, as I cannot admit that our free will is reduced to nothing, I imagine that it may be true that fortune disposes of half of our actions, but that it leaves more or less the other half in our power. I compare it to an impetuous river which, when it overflows, floods the plains, topples trees and buildings, removes land from one side and carries it to another: everything flees before its ravages, everything yields to its fury; nothing can stop it. Nevertheless, however fearsome it may be, once the storm has passed, people try to protect themselves from it by building dykes, causeways and other works, so that when new floods occur, the waters are contained within a channel and can no longer spread so freely and cause such great devastation. The same is true of fortune, which shows its power above all where no resistance has been prepared, and brings its fury to bear where it knows there is no obstacle ready to stop it.

If we consider Italy, which is the theatre and source of the great changes we have seen and are seeing taking place, we will find that it resembles a vast countryside unprotected by any kind of defence. If it had been protected, like Germany, Spain and France, against the torrent, it would not have been flooded, or at least it would not have suffered as much.

Limiting myself to these general ideas about the resistance that can be put up against fortune, and moving on to more specific observations, I note first of all that it is not unusual to see a prince prosper one day and fall the next, without nevertheless having changed either his character or his conduct. This comes, it seems to me, from what I have already established at some length, that a prince who relies entirely on fortune falls as fortune varies. It also seems to me that a prince is happy or unhappy, depending on whether or not his conduct is in keeping with the times in which he reigns. All men have the same goal in mind: glory and riches; but they do not all act in the same way in everything that is aimed at achieving this goal: some proceed with circumspection, others with impetuosity; some use violence, others artifice; some are patient, others not at all: these different ways of acting, though very different, can be equally successful. We see, moreover, that of two men who follow the same course, one arrives and the other does not; whereas, on the contrary, two others who walk very differently, and, for example, one with circumspection and the other with impetuosity, nevertheless arrive equally at their end: and where does this come from, if not from the fact that the ways of proceeding are or are not in accordance with the times? This is what causes two different actions to produce the same effect, and two similar actions to have opposite results. This is also why what is good is not always good. Thus, for example, a prince governs with circumspection and patience: if the nature and circumstances of the times are such that this way of governing is good, he will prosper; but he will fail, on the contrary, if, as the nature and circumstances of the times change, he does not himself change his system.

Even the most prudent men do not know how to change at the right moment, either because they cannot act against their own character, or because, once they have prospered for a long time by following a certain path, they cannot persuade themselves that it is a good idea to take another. So the circumspect man, not knowing how to be impetuous when he should, is himself the architect of his own ruin. If we could change our character according to time and circumstance, fortune would never change.

Pope Julius II acted with impetuosity in all his endeavours, and this way of acting was so in keeping with the times and circumstances that the result was always a happy one. Consider his first undertaking, the one he carried out on Bologna during the lifetime of Messer Giovanni Bentivogli: the

Venetians took a dim view of it, and it was a subject of discussion for Spain and France; nevertheless, Julius rushed into it with his natural resolution and impetuosity, leading the expedition himself; and, by this boldness, he kept the Venetians and Spain at bay, so that no one moved: The Venetians, because they feared, and Spain, because it wished to recover the kingdom of Naples in its entirety. Moreover, he drew the King of France to his aid; for this monarch, seeing that the Pope had set off on his march, and wishing to win his friendship, which he needed to bring down the Venetians, judged that he could not refuse him the help of his troops without clearly offending him. Julius therefore obtained, through his impetuosity, what another would not have obtained with all human prudence; for if he had waited to leave Rome, as any other pope would have done, until everything had been agreed, decided and prepared, he certainly would not have succeeded. The King of France would have found a thousand ways to apologise to him, and the other powers would have found just as many to frighten him.

I will not speak here of the other operations of this pontiff, which, all conducted in the same way, were equally successful. Moreover, the brevity of his life did not allow him to experience the setbacks he would probably have suffered if he had lived in a time when it would have been necessary to behave with circumspection; for he would never have been able to abandon the system of violence to which his character only too often led him.

I conclude, therefore, that as fortune changes, and men persist in the same way of acting, they are happy as long as this way agrees with fortune; but as soon as this agreement ceases, they become unhappy.

I think, moreover, that it is better to be impetuous than circumspect; for fortune is a woman: to keep her submissive, you have to treat her roughly; she yields rather to men who use violence than to those who act coldly: so she is always a friend of young men, who are less reserved, more impetuous, and who command more boldly.

Chapter XXVI: Exhortation to deliver Italy from the barbarians.

Reflecting on all that I have set out above, and examining for myself whether today the times would be such in Italy that a new prince could make himself illustrious there, and whether a prudent and courageous man would find the opportunity and the means to give this country a new form, It seems to me that so many circumstances conspire in favour of such a plan that I do not know if there has ever been a more propitious time than this for these great changes.

And if, as I have said, it was necessary for the people of Israel to be slaves to the Egyptians in order to know the virtue of Moses; if the greatness of Cyrus's soul could only shine forth as long as the Persians were oppressed by the Medes; if, finally, in order to appreciate the full value of Theseus, it was necessary for the Athenians to be disunited : In the same way, in those days, for any genius to shine, Italy had to be reduced to the point where it is now; it had to be more oppressed than the Hebrews, more enslaved than the Persians, more disunited than the Athenians, without leaders, without institutions, beaten, torn apart, invaded, and overwhelmed by every kind of disaster.

Until now, a few glimmers of light have occasionally appeared to herald a man chosen by God for her deliverance; but soon she saw this man stopped by fortune in his brilliant career, and she is still waiting, almost dying, for the one who will be able to close her wounds, put an end to the pillage and plunder suffered by Lombardy, put an end to the exactions and vexations that plague the kingdom of Naples and Tuscany, and finally heal her wounds that are so inveterate that they have become fistulous.

We also see her constantly praying to heaven to deign to send her someone to deliver her from the cruelty and insolence of the barbarians. We also see her ready and willing to rally under the first banner that someone dares to unfurl before her eyes. But where better to place her hopes than in your illustrious House, which, through its hereditary virtues, its fortune, the favour of God and that of the Church, whose throne it currently occupies, can truly lead and bring about this happy deliverance.

It will not be difficult, if you have before you the life and deeds of these heroes whom I have just named. They were, it is true, rare and marvellous men; but they were men after all; and the opportunities they seized were less favourable than the present one. Their undertakings were no more just than this one, and they had no more protection from heaven than you do. This is where justice shines in all its glory, for war is always just when it is necessary, and arms are sacred when they are the only resource of the oppressed. Here, all the wishes of the people call to you; and, in the midst of this unanimous disposition, success cannot be uncertain: all you have to do is follow the example of those whom I have proposed to you as models.

Moreover, God manifests his will by striking signs: the sea was parted, a luminous cloud showed the way, the rock caused waters to gush forth from its bosom, manna fell in the desert; everything thus favours your greatness. Let the rest be your work: God does not want to do everything, so as not to leave us without merit and without that portion of glory which he allows us to acquire.

That none of the Italians of whom I have spoken has been able to do what is expected of your illustrious house; that even in the midst of so many revolutions that Italy has undergone, and of so many wars of which it has been the theatre, it seemed that all military valour had been extinguished, is nothing to be surprised about: this is because the old institutions were bad, and there was no one who knew how to find new ones. There is nothing, however, that does more honour to a man who is beginning to rise than to have been able to introduce new laws and new institutions: if these laws and these institutions are based on a solid foundation, and if they have greatness, they make him admired and respected by all men.

Italy, moreover, offers a subject capable of the most universal reforms. It is here that courage will shine forth in every individual, provided that the leaders themselves do not lack it. See in duels and battles between a small number of opponents how superior the Italians are in strength, skill and intelligence. But if they fight as an army, all their value vanishes. On the one hand, those who know are not obedient, and everyone thinks they know; on the other, there has been no leader high enough, either through personal merit or fortune, above the others, for everyone to recognise his superiority and submit to him. As a result, for so long, and during so many wars that have taken place over the last twenty years, any army composed entirely of Italians has suffered nothing but setbacks, first witnessing the Taro, then Alexandria, Capua, Genoa, Vailà, Cologne and Mestri.

If your illustrious house wishes to imitate the great men who, at different times, delivered their country, what it must do first of all, and what must be the basis of its enterprise, is to provide itself with national forces, for they are the strongest, the most loyal and the best that can be possessed: each of the soldiers who make them up, being good personally, will become even better when all together see themselves commanded, honoured and maintained by their prince. It is with weapons like these that Italian valour will be able to repel foreigners.

The Swiss infantry and the Spanish infantry are considered to be terrible; but there is such a flaw in both that it is possible to form a third, capable not only of resisting them, but also of defeating them. Indeed, the Spanish infantry cannot stand up to the cavalry, and the Swiss infantry must fear any other troops of the same nature who will fight with the same obstinacy as it. We have also seen, and will see again, the French cavalry defeat the Spanish infantry, and the latter destroy the Swiss infantry; of which there has been, if not a complete experience, at least a test in the battle of Ravenna, where the Spanish infantry found itself at odds with the German battalions, which observe the same discipline as the Swiss: We saw the Spaniards, favoured by their agility and covered by their small shields, penetrate under the lances into the ranks of their adversaries, striking them without risk and without the Germans being able to prevent them; and they would have destroyed them to the last, if the cavalry had not come to charge them themselves in turn.

Now that we know the shortcomings of these two types of infantry, we can organise a new one that can withstand cavalry and not fear other foot soldiers. It is not necessary to create a new type of troop; it is enough to find a new organisation, a new way of fighting; and it is through such inventions that a new prince acquires reputation and succeeds in growing.

Let us not, therefore, miss this opportunity. May Italy, after such a long wait, at last see her liberator appear! I cannot find words to express with what love, with what thirst for vengeance, with what unshakeable loyalty, with what veneration and tears of joy he would be received in all the provinces that have suffered so much from these floods of foreigners! What doors could remain closed to him? What peoples would refuse to obey him? What jealousy would stand in the way of his success? What Italian would not surround him with respect? Is there anyone whose heart would not leap at the thought of barbarian domination?

May your illustrious house take upon itself this noble burden with the courage and hope of success that a just and legitimate undertaking inspires; may, under its banner, the common homeland recover its ancient splendour, and may, under its auspices, these verses of Petrarch finally come to fruition!

"Virtù contra furore

Prenderà l'arme, e fia'l combatter corto;

Che l'antico valore

Negl'italici cor non è ancor morto."

Petrarca, Canz. XVI, V. 93-96

END OF THE PRINCE.

1. See the note at the end of the Prince.

2. Despite this reticence, Machiavelli speaks very distinctly about republics, in chapter V among others. M. Artaud thinks that this passage was subjected to censorship, and consequently altered, when the Medici allowed this book to be printed.

3. Machiavelli returns to this thought several times; he says again in Book IV of the History of Florence: "As for powerful men, either they must not be touched, or when they are touched, they must be killed". This maxim is one of those that have been most fiercely attacked.

4. Frederick II, in chapter VI of the Antimachiavel, says about this passage:

"It seems to me that Machiavelli places Moses rather inconsiderately with Romulus, Cyrus and Theseus. Either Moses was inspired or he was not. If he was not, which we must not suppose, then he could only be regarded as an impostor who used God, in much the same way as poets use their gods as machines when they lack a climax. Moreover, Moses was so unskilled at human reasoning that he led the Jewish people for forty years on a journey they could have made in six weeks; he had benefited very little from the enlightenment of the Egyptians, and in this sense he was far inferior to Romulus, Theseus and those heroes. If Moses was inspired by God, as can be seen in everything, he can only be regarded as the blind organ of divine omnipotence; and the leader of the Jews was in this sense far inferior, as a man, to the founder of the Roman Empire, to the monarch of the Persians and to the heroes who did, by their own valour and strength, greater deeds than the other did with the immediate assistance of God".

5. Col gesso, a word from Alexander VI, meaning that King Charles had nothing more to do than to have a marshal mark the lodgings on the doors with chalk.

6. The idea of substituting national troops for mercenary troops was developed at length by Machiavelli, in books I and II of his treatise on the Art of War. For an appreciation of our author, as a tactician, see Colonel Carion-Nisas: Essai sur l'histoire de l'art militaire, Paris, 1824, chap. II, of Machiavelli considered as a military writer and observer of the state of Europe, in terms of war, at the end of the Middle Ages. Count Algarotti, a friend of Frederick II, also wrote a work on the Seven Books of the Art of War.

7. The author is referring to Ferdinand the Catholic, King of Aragon and Castile.